It's All About CUSTOMERS!

JOHN FRAZER-ROBINSON

It's All About CUSTOMERS!

The Perfect way to

GROW YOUR BUSINESS

through Marketing,

Sales and Service

INSTITUTE OF DIRECTORS

KOGAN
PAGE

First published as *Customer-Driven Marketing* in 1997

Second edition published as *It's All About Customers!* in 1999

Kogan Page Limited
120 Pentonville Road
London N1 9JN

British Library Cataloguing in Publication Data

A CIP record for this book is available from the British Library.

ISBN 0 7494 3073 7

Typeset by Kogan Page
Printed and bound in Great Britain by Bell & Bain Ltd, Glasgow

Contents

Dedication

This book is dedicated to my wife Elaine whose hard work, help, energy and drive are always invaluable and motivational.

Elaine and I share a very real passion for ethical business practices, sound management methods and a belief in change, growth and personal development as a way of business and personal life. We both love our personal achievements to come through helping others to achieve.

Thank you for all your support with so many things and in so many ways. And, as ever, all my love to you.

Acknowledgements

Pip Mosscrop: Pip, many thanks for your thoughts, help and guidance. And it's good to have you there to work with, to talk to and to debate what's going on – and as ever to put the world to rights!

Andy Macmillan and Saadia Asis: Andy proved a brilliant researcher for much of the early part of my work and considerably facilitated my path and direction. Saadia, whom we found at Exeter Business School, helped with the more recent research and provided me not only with an extra pair of eyes to catch up on the reading, but also an astute sense in her synopsis writing. I pay tribute to you both. I am sure you will do well in your respective careers. I shall cheer you on!

Andrew Wilson, The Catalogue Consultancy: Andrew kindly agreed to read and discuss elements of the book prior to publishing. Thanks Andrew (and Marianne!) for obliging with your time and your valued opinion.

To IBM's Communications Library, Rank Xerox, Olivetti, Royal Insurance; to London & Manchester Assurance – particularly Lawrence Smith and Derek Hall; to Karsten Wijk and other friends at Mölnlycke in Sweden and throughout Europe; to my many long-time and valued friends at Royal Mail; to the energetic and exciting team at Hollard in South Africa; and to all those others who have shared their stories with me (or Andy); to all those other valued Clients, colleagues and friends who have given me the opportunity to assist with their problems (and learn some more about the meaning of life).

And to all those kind people who let me use, abuse or mess with their material...yes, to each and every one of you...thank you.

About this book

This is a management book about turning your business into a Customer-focused organization. Not in the shallow cosmetic way that enables businesses to pay lip service to Customer service – but in a real way. It is also a book about making your business more efficient, driving costs down and re-focusing, particularly but not exclusively, your marketing, sales and service around the Customer.

I have met many, many people – managers, directors and proprietors – who believe they run Customer-driven businesses because they care about their Customers and give good service. These same people are actually running businesses that have only scratched the surface of becoming Customer-driven. As a result, in blissful ignorance, they are enjoying only a portion of the benefits and profits.

This is a management book from a marketing perspective. Throughout, marketing is seen as a culture rather than a department or another word for sales. Marketing is a function, but Customer-driven marketing is also a way of doing business. Often in the pages ahead, I wanted to write 'marketing, sales, advertising and service' – sometimes, for clarity, I have. However, in most cases, I have just used the term 'marketing', which refers to the marketing of your business in the widest possible context. The view in this book is that marketing encompasses sales and advertising and most of the aspects of Customer service.

This is a book about making money. It shows you how to maximize profits through the following passionate belief:

> The object of a business is not to make money.
> The object of a business is to serve its Customers.
> The result is to make money.

Preface

The WOW Factor

Let me tell you about the WOW Factor. It started in Johannesburg where I had been working with the enterprising Hollard Insurance Group. I worked with Hollard to invent and launch Direct Solutions. Over there on a trip to review progress prior to the launch, the project team ran their plans past me. 'What do you think?' they asked. 'It's OK,' I ventured, 'but it's got no WOW. I thought we were aiming to make every transaction or Customer interaction more than special. Surely, we are going for WOW? Every time we do something for a Customer, it should make them go "WOW".'

The WOW thing at Hollard went on to become a very big deal. It drove every future decision that the project group made. At every stage we checked for WOW! If it wasn't there, we established what WOW would be from the Customer's point of view, and then put it there.

I was explaining the WOW Factor to a workshop audience in Dubai when Masoud Mohammed Saleh, head of the Dubai Department of Civil Aviation marketing team, told me he had a WOW story. Masoud's tale made our whole group go 'WOW!' See what you think...

Masoud, his wife and their infant child were in the progress of an almost-round-the-world trip with the airline Lufthansa. Arriving at Frankfurt – about half-way through the itinerary – he secured his own bag and his wife's from the belt. But the brightly coloured rucksack belonging to the little one was not there. A baggage handler, spotting their plight, hurried off to find the supervisor from Lufthansa. She arrived. 'What was in the bag, Sir?'

'Actually, not much,' replied Masoud, 'but it was important. The baby's milk for the trip and Pampers.' The Lufthansa rep asked some more questions, including, rather curiously, the baby's doctor's phone number in Dubai. Masoud, puzzled, obliged with the number.

Ten minutes passed. Back came the Lufthansa rep with the airline's Frankfurt Manager of Customer Service. 'Sorry we took so long,' they explained, 'but we wanted to call your doctor because we don't have the brand of milk your baby drinks here. This one he has approved. And here is a box of Pampers. Make the baby comfortable, then we'll go and buy a nice new bag.' You might think 'Well done, Lufthansa', but that was just the beginning.

For the rest of the trip, at every destination, Masoud and his family were treated to free Pampers and a free supply of milk approved by their family doctor. Again you might think, 'Well done, Lufthansa', but it wasn't over yet.

The airline said 'we fixed the problem, but we haven't said sorry yet. We have decided your baby will enjoy a 75 per cent ticket discount for life.' WOW!

If you think about this, it is a great win/win situation. The result was seriously impressed Customers, for whom Lufthansa will be the family's first choice for decades. First, as the parents accompany the child, and then, as the child becomes an adult, and then a parent with his or her own partner and little ones.

You'll find more stories in this book of people who are making their Customers go 'WOW!' Yet companies find it hard to make every Customer interaction a WOW interaction. And the bigger the company, the harder it seems. It may seem harder, indeed it may be harder, but read on and you'll see that it can certainly be achieved.

I have seen some absolute miracles come to pass. And I am beginning to see these miracles with more and more regularity. They happen around people who are prepared to think big, accept that the past was yesterday and realize that what worked then will not work today because it is no longer suitable, no longer effective, no longer valid. These are the kind of people who would understand why I wrote and pinned this legend to my office wall: 'If it ain't broke, fix it!'

And actually that's where I believe today's business world has currently settled down. We've seen and survived the days of 'If it ain't broke, don't fix it'; we've seen and endured the slightly scary days of 'If it ain't broke, break it'; now here we are trying to cope with a relentless, unpredictable change-crazy world, in which we have to be ready with the solution after next, just before we have diagnosed the problem before last. So, if it ain't broke, fix it!

Assess your chances of survival

Actually, what we are talking about here is corporate survival. You can easily rate yourself and the business you are in. Run down the following list, scoring five as 'excellent' and zero as 'may not last the year'! Take a look at your business, the people around you and your present workload, then tot up your score. You really can determine whether your business will be in business in five, ten or even fifteen years time when you ask yourself these questions:

- Do you feel as if you are constructing the future of your business (5); or merely tinkering with the present (0)?
- Are you and your team more worried about what you can make happen this time next year – or even the year after (5); or about your present problems (0)?
- Are you truly giving your competitors something to think about (5); or are you just another business following along with the crowd (0)?
- Are you dedicated to redesigning your business to have a strategy that leaves your competitors on the starting blocks (5); or are you simply trying to fix the old problems, breakdowns and failures (0)?
- Are you perceived by Customers and competitors as ground-breakers (5); or followers (0)?
- How much of your personal work time is concerned with discovering tomorrow's opportunities (5); how much with resolving yesterday's hangovers (0)?
- Among all the employees in your business does there exist commitment, energy, belief and excitement (5); or stress, anxiety, uncertainty and a sense of being out of control of their own destiny (0)?
- Is the future of your business being fashioned by the directors' unique perception, dream or vision (5); or are you being driven to create new products and services, new methods and new standards and turnarounds by your competitors (0)?
- Do you face most days with a smile and look forward to the years ahead, staying with the company (5); or is work quite often a drudge, and are you thinking of moving on to somewhere where you are more appreciated (0)?

If you score less than 35 out of the 45 possible, you are at risk. To be specific, you are at risk because the future of your business is at risk.

Businesses whose employees answer those questions and score less than 35 are destined only ever to reach the heady heights of mediocrity. Those businesses are content to let their people wallow, and to allow their position to be less than highly competitive; those businesses don't realize or don't care that you can out-smart and out-think a good deal of change; in effect, those businesses are leaving their future to chance. If you are any good at all, get out of there! If you own it, sell it. Quickly.

All of this serves to endorse the hard lesson that really should not be a surprise to any of us. It explains exactly why yesterday's solutions won't work any more. Even today's solutions are struggling! Technology is moving so fast; competitive edges and product life-cycles have become so short; the business climate and environment is changing so rapidly; and Customer expectations have reached such sophistication.

I often explain to people that what the Customer wants has changed from pies to pasta. Those who sit around trying to get their pie machine (that's their existing sales, advertising, marketing and Customer service processes in this analogy) to make pasta will waste a lot of corporate time, effort, resource and money. They will not experience any miracles. Those who have created, or who will soon begin to create pasta machines, get to go for the breakthroughs and miracles. But there's no getting away from the fact that pie machines can't make pasta any more than the old-style businesses, cultures and processes can cope with the new style of business.

To continue the analogy, the next question, of course, is which shapes should the pasta from your new machine be! Well, that depends on what your Customers tell you they want. And the answers from your own Customers will be different, sometimes subtly, sometimes not so subtly, from those from your competitors' Customers. But they will always be different – which is why the days when we could take other people's business solutions and use them to solve our own problems have gone. Nowadays, we have to find our own solutions. If you hang around waiting to see what the others do, you get overtaken and often at the speed of light. It's getting harder out there, not easier. This is a point with which we will keep coming face to face!

Breakthroughs are BIG! But they don't always bring miracles

Breakthroughs are big and to qualify as breakthroughs they should make big differences. I can't tell you the number of times I sit around with pleasant, well-meaning people who want to discuss things that will make tiny differences to sales volumes and tiny differences to market share. No chance of a breakthrough. No miracles will happen for them.

Yet, I vividly remember a story which an American friend and fellow conference speaker, Murray Raphael, once told me. It so affected me that I went out and tried the idea his story contained with another friend at the very next opportunity. I won't tell you Murray's original story, but I will share the personal experience.

I had a friend some years ago who was in a retail business. We were having lunch on my birthday, which happens to be a few days after New Year. We sat in a Sussex pub chatting. In view of the season, I asked him what he felt his business prospects were for the year ahead. Britain was in the grip of recession. His answer was gloomy. 'Well,' he mused, 'I figure I'll do well just to hit this year's figures again.' No breakthroughs there – not a miracle in sight!

Then, the magic question (thank you, Murray). I asked him 'Can I ask you, if it were possible to lift your business by, say, 20 per cent, what do you think you'd have to do?'

Within ten minutes we had potential breakthroughs all around us. At least eight viable and, it seemed, achievable ideas. Real potential miracles. His whole spirit lifted and he couldn't wait to finish lunch and get started. Weeks later when I visited his store, the buzz, the energy, were vividly at work. This was a business that was going somewhere.

I can tell you what happened. Business went up around 16 per cent. He improved his sales productivity by about the same again by realigning his staffing and changing his opening hours. Costs dropped by eight per cent at a time when inflation was high. Of the eight potential miracles, five failed or made no discernible difference. Three initiatives succeeded. Three real breakthroughs occurred, three miracles took place.

Are there some breakthroughs and miracles promised to you in this book?

I am privileged to work at the leading edge of what's happening. It's risky. It's fun. It's scary. It's exciting. It's where the breakthroughs and the miracles happen. However, I should explain, for this book it has a cost. Often, as a speaker, people ask you for results, facts and, most of all, case histories. They want to know what's happening to people that is new. They want me to tell them what is happening that is exciting and working. Actually, they want me to say, in effect, 'It's OK. Others have been here before you. It's quite safe.' The truth is, if others have been here before you, you've been overtaken. It's too late.

Most of my Clients are experimenting. Each time we seem to move nearer and nearer a solution, the question changes. Case histories are just that – history. If you want a book that abounds, like so many others, in revealing details of the inner machinations of huge companies, by all means buy one. But you must realize this: it will be a history book.

This is no apology!

I'm not apologizing! The fact is, I'd rather feel free to tell you an anonymous story or share an anonymous experience than not tell or share it at all. Indeed, I sometimes take the view that if it's old enough to be openly told, it's too late to learn something vitally new from it. That's not strictly true. But it does tell you which bits to watch out for…and, often, of which bits I'm most proud!

I know you would love to know! However, the people who pay me seem not to mind me sharing with you the things I do with them, but they naturally and reasonably fear their competitors – and that's possibly you – knowing too much about what they are doing. Competitive edges are getting harder to create and sustain, not easier! This means that, often for good and very valid contractual reasons, they are reluctant to set me free to tell you who, or in which country, they are. They will probably, however, recognize themselves!

I respect and understand your thirst for information. What I can share with you, I will. I'll still tell the stories and, I promise you, wherever I can, the names and places. Frustratingly, with the really interesting stuff, that's rare. But it happened or it is happening. It's out there – a breakthrough together with its accompanying miracle – to challenge, stimulate, motivate and excite you.

Making your breakthroughs and miracles

You may be wondering what constitutes a breakthrough – or, for that matter, a miracle? Miracles to me are huge uplifts in sales productivity: one of my Clients is going for 300 per cent in three years. Miracles to me are massive shifts in the ROI (Return on Investment) offered by marketing. I have several Clients experiencing 30 to 40 per cent improvements. Some are spending less now with the same volume results. Some are redeploying the money elsewhere and going for increased growth. Some are using the savings to improve Customer communications and create long-term Customer loyalty strategies and activities. Each one of these I would consider a real miracle. The breakthroughs behind these are nearly always changes in thinking and attitude; often, later, of course, they lead to changes in method or process.

In this book we can find breakthroughs together. We can make miracles. This is not idle bragging. My role as a consultant is not to impose my solutions on people but to facilitate them creating and owning their own miracles. They, my Clients, carry the accolades as far as I'm concerned. Otherwise, neither the breakthroughs nor miracles actually happen. However, such big things may not always come easily.

Will you really find your own breakthroughs and miracles in this book?

Hopefully you will. For this book contains the information that will enable you to create miracles. It tells how others have achieved miracles. But it does not provide you with ready-made solutions. The future does not recognize those words – 'ready-made solutions' – any more. This is a book about the future of business. It has a great emphasis on marketing, sales and Customer service. This is a book that explains how those three functions or activities are now one. This is a book that preaches that the practice of 'thinking Customer' should reach into every nook and cranny of your organization as well as deep into the hearts, minds and souls of every individual who works in it. And I do mean everyone. This is, above all, a book about thinking quality before quantity. This is a book about why and how and what happens if you really do go for a miracle.

What happens if you don't create your own breakthroughs and miracles? Not a pleasant thought. But at least the words 'long lingering death' are not seen very often in the business community these days.

Corporate deaths are much quicker now and often far more spectacular too!

Make no mistake, I say again, the future is harder, not easier. It is fraught with problems – most of all, in my view, for the marketing, sales and Customer service people and processes. Sadly, they've been the slowest off the blocks and need all the miracles they can get. I hope such people will feel, by the end of this book, that they can see where the breakthroughs will come for them. And how to achieve them.

However this is not just a book for marketing, sales and Customer service managers and directors. It is for MDs and CEOs too. It is for management of all levels and every specialization. For businesses large or small. It is about survival and success in the Age of the Customer. When your business (or the business you are in) wins, you win. No business can win unless everyone in it is working for the Customer, and understands why this has to be so. From the accounts department, to the shopfloor, to buying, to the front line. Every single company person must be, in part or in whole, a Customer person. Why? Because, if business seems to have forgotten one thing in the last thirty years, it's this: it's all about Customers.

1

The false premise of excellence and quality

Do you work in a quality business? Or a quantity business? Is it possible to work for a business that is both?

Since Peters and Waterman first wrote *In Search of Excellence* in 1982, the business world is alleged to have been heading towards a quality age. The fact is, back in 1990, when I wrote *Total Quality Marketing*, there was little evidence to show that quality standards overall were really improving. Nowadays, I am privileged to work as a consultant with a number of firms that have made the link that quality matters and is the path to survival, if not for ever, at least for a good decade or two. Yet the number of companies throughout the world that are deeply committed to quality, and see it as a vital strand to delivering beyond Customer expectations, is still small. For most, it seems they are simply managing to regain lost ground rather than actually to improve quality.

You see, I come from the Jaundiced School that says, 'If Man does not have a great enough perception of what quality is, then no amount of training can teach those who are deficient in appreciation of such standards to deliver them.' More, if you examine the Excellence and Quality movements in detail, you will see that what they really offer is to turn back the clock, applying the standards of bygone days to today's profit-based material age.

The premise is that if you get back to product supremacy through quality, you cannot fail. Sadly, it is an entirely false premise –

undeniably noble, but entirely false. No miracles there. For it would only work well if we were indeed living in a truly quality business age; sadly, however, despite it being fashionable for almost a decade or so, we are not. We are living today in a transitional age – the crossover time between quantity and quality. Not that they are absolutely mutually exclusive. But they are, I fear, a lot more so than the Excellence or the Total Quality brigade would have had us believe.

Some, possibly even you, may think these views extreme. Then take off your business hat and ask yourself, as a consumer, how many genuine quality businesses do you know? If you can think of one, perhaps even two or three, where you are constantly and consistently super-impressed, not just with what they do but *how* they do it, you are doing well. You have seen the WOW Factor at work. You may have glimpsed a miracle. And my guess is that you will be thinking of a business that puts its relationship building substantially in front of making the next sale.

These are the kind of businesses that share one of my philosophies about Customers: that it's far better to concentrate on what you do *for* Customers than what you do *to* Customers.

These businesses put Customers in front of everything. Obvious examples are those one-man bands, relics of the age of craftsmen. They do a job for you at home, they are a pleasure to deal with, leave no mess, make a skilled and exemplary job of the task, and charge a fair price...a miracle! But have you noticed how it nearly always takes you weeks, or even months, to get hold of them because they truly find it difficult to meet the demand. Of course! There is only the one of them. Yet, if they should want to grow...and, oddly, few of them do!...how could they do it? Indeed, could they do it at all without jeopardizing their standards?

At the other end of the scale, multi-national corporations, those who, basically driven by greed as opposed to growth, first abandoned these quality ethics for quantity, scale and size (and set us fair and square along 30 to 40 years of exploitation selling to deliver almost entirely to quantity based objectives) are now seeking to go into reverse thrust. Except, of course, many are still being run by quantity-minded materialists, men and women who have climbed the corporate tree during the last 20 years or so; they find it difficult to shake off the old ways. Which is where the gurus of Excellence and the dragomans of Total Quality come in. These are businesses waiting for miracles to come along. But they don't just happen by like that.

One to the power of the people

I well remember a greetings card I received from a friend, a management consultant whom I respect greatly. A few days after I left the corporate world to become a self-employed consultant, his message dropped on my mat. It said, 'Congratulations! You are now the perfect size for a business.' And he was absolutely right. Again, my views might be considered somewhat extreme, but I maintain that a business with 4,000 staff will find it literally 4,000 times harder to be Customer-responsive, Customer-focused and Customer-caring. Indeed, the moment a business grows from one to two, the rot sets in.

The fact is that a business with 4,000 people, in order to achieve and maintain a competitive stance as a Customer-focused, Customer-responsive business, has to cultivate and grow that Customer mentality and attitude in each and every employee. *Every* staff member has to make Customer-first decisions *all* the time: down to when they take their lunch, how they answer the phone, how late they work and when they take their holidays. Getting a business of hundreds or thousands of people all to be Customer people, all making Customer-first decisions, all 100 per cent on-side, is incredibly difficult – which is why it is equally rare!

Despite all the new technology, the improvement in databases, the mind-blowing and laudable rise of call centres, and other magic Customer service-enhancing devices, companies still frequently fail their Customers. And the reason is not so often that the computer system has gone down (although that happens frequently enough!), it is mostly because the culture, or philosophy, or ideal, has gone down. When this happens, it is a people issue, a human issue.

Oh, please let me go on being your Customer!

Let me give you an example of a people issue.

There were just two hours to go before my wife and I were due to set off for a week away on speaking assignments in Spain and the Philippines. We'd been back from South Africa for less than two days, just long enough to clear some messages, pick up our slides and equipment, grab some sleep, unpack and re-pack. Then we were off. Our housekeeper, Lin, had offered to run us to the airport in my car. Suddenly, I realized, since I had changed my car a few months earlier, I had not included Lin as a named driver on the insurance policy. Panic!

I rang the insurance broker, got through to the call centre, and gave my policy number. The agent paused a few seconds, waiting for her screen to load up with my record, and then told me, 'Your policy was terminated 17 days ago.'

No, it can't have been! Otherwise I've been driving round illegally, uninsured. 'Yes, Sir, that's correct. You have.'

I didn't need this. I explained the situation in full, somewhat testily, but the telephone agent kept her cool. 'Don't worry, Sir,' she reassured me. 'I'll transfer you to the quotations team and we'll have a new policy in force within minutes.'

'No you won't!', I told her, 'because I don't fit your system.'

Let me tell you what had happened. When I first bought my present car, I rang to advise the broker of the change. They replied that my new vehicle was over the value covered by their contract with the insurer so they would have to get me a new quote. They did. The best they could find was four times the premium I had been paying.

As luck would have it, not only had I helped to launch this brokerage when it was founded many years before by a leading motoring organization, the general manager at the time, an old friend, had become managing director. Coincidentally, he had moved on to become chairman. I decided to call him. The result was, as I had thought it might be, that of course they didn't want to lose my increased business. A call was made to the broker instructing them that, for a reasonably increased premium of about 20 per cent, they should accept my business. You would think, from the tone of the call that I received from the broker, that I had done something truly underhand, disgusting and possibly even criminal. All I had said to the insurer was, 'I've been with you nine years, I really want to go on being insured by you. Please will you go on taking my money!'

Back to the hectic morning – there are now less than 90 minutes until we're due to head off to Heathrow airport. I still have three to four hours' work to do. The little hair I have left is in danger of being torn out. Someone else is now accessing the computer system to get me a quote. 'You're wasting your time!' I tell her. 'My car is valued in excess of the amount covered by your agreement with the insurer.'

'I have now put your details into the system, Sir. I have to advise you that your car is in excess of the value covered by our agreement with the insurer.'

Growl.

'But don't worry. I'll put you through to our special underwriting department...'. I could finish this one for her. It would go like this: '...who will come up with a quote which is four times higher than the premium you presently pay!' I was in the 'system' loop, and I was at boiling point. Only then did it occur to me to find out why they had terminated the policy in the first place. This was, after all, not a problem of my making. I asked to speak to a supervisor. The policy had been terminated because I hadn't paid the extra premium that had been necessary when I changed vehicles. But I hadn't been asked for it. They had failed to notify me of, and ask me for, the amount due. And, to be quite candid, I had totally forgotten about it. 'However, Sir,' a curt voice informed me, 'we sent you a recorded delivery letter before we terminated the policy and you still failed to respond.'

Now we go into the postal saga. I had not received a letter by recorded delivery. Even though we travel and are away from home a great deal, and, living in a 400-year-old house, don't have a letterbox, we do have an 'arrangement' with the local post office 30 metres away. Betty, the postmistress, gathers our mail and, if needs be, signs for it too. There was no way a recorded delivery letter could have arrived without being signed for. Richard, our postman, quickly cottoned on to the amount of mail I get from Royal Mail Strategic Headquarters, and 'looks after' me (which, actually, in this rural community, he would have done anyway). I explained all that. The call-centre supervisor was at last lost for words. Actually, I was speechless myself!

How was I going to get around this one? I had only 55 minutes left, at least 15 of which would be needed to pack my work into my briefcase to handle in the airport lounge. Eureka! I rang my old friend at the insurer.

He had retired. However, full marks to his successor, who asked someone to ring the broker. With 20 minutes to spare, my policy was reinstated and the outstanding premium was paid using a credit card.

It seems to be so hard to give people your business and your money sometimes! But why?

Why should a Customer lose when the system wins?

I would be very surprised if you, or anyone else who picks up this book, hadn't had a similar sort of experience. Believe me, everyone who attends my sessions on 'Customer-driven Marketing' always has at least one nightmare tale to tell. Often, they can relate two or three. They range from tales about banks to airlines to holiday companies to mail order businesses to the inevitable insurance companies. And it seems that, the more 'technologized' we become, the more woeful tales are.

This may not be true. It may simply be that the more we become used to the increasingly improving service, the more the apparently insane anomalies stand out. So here's the point for me. In my example the system was working just fine. What was failing was the human element. That unique ability we have as human beings to say 'that doesn't make any sense'. That capacity to exercise our right to be more intelligent than the artificial intelligence (even if this may not last much longer!).

Here is a truly ironic incompatibility; one of those glorious paradoxes life so tantalizingly and constantly dangles before us! The very technology that is supposed to be helping us deal with Customers on a genuine one-to-one basis actually functions best when there is the maximum homogeneity between those Customers. Believe me, until this one is resolved, there will be an increasing role for the human touch to make sense of things. We consumers are being told that we are allowed to be more and more different. We can have more and more choices and preferences, which widen further and further our differences, and support our feelings of individuality. Meanwhile 'systems' constantly try to deny it all, shove us back into the drab box of uniformity and close the lid on us.

Later, you will read that I place much emphasis on these emotional and human aspects of the business – the 'soft' issues, as I call them. If we believe that Customer relationships are important, we must increasingly understand, respect, and pay tribute to our Customers' feelings.

Quick, quick, slow down!

Let's return to quality. When people crow about BS 5750 or DIN 9000, what are they saying? Are they saying that, despite the absurd bureaucracy, they are committed to the very highest levels of performance? Why do so many ads and commercials and letterheads celebrate these certifications? There are no miracles here, I assure you. Aren't they, after all, simply a set of basic minimum standards? Frankly, any business that doesn't qualify for them doesn't deserve to be in business.

Yes, we are now finally beginning the headlong dash into the Age of the Customer. But what a pity! Because if ever a directional change needed deep, reflective thought and time, this is the one.

Many people will say, 'Wake up to reality. Our business doesn't have time to stand still and think.' Who mentioned standing still? Let's think on our feet. Let's by all means act 'Customer' now – but let's also recognize what this means.

For those involved in selling – and I cast the net as wide as it can be flung – this is a mammoth task. Selling has, it seems, been quantity-driven since time began; but, in the last 40 years, it has become quantity-obsessed. This obsession has, in my view, led to practices and standards that can barely be justified. There is no mitigation. We are all to blame.

The judge and jury are beginning to deliberate, and will continue over the coming years, until they come to pronounce sentence. Our Customers are our judge and jury and, following a period of relative peace and affluence in much of the civilized world, they have come to realize that they have the money. Therefore, they call the tune.

Now that we have a 'global village' created by the media, there are no little comfortable corners to hide. What a shopper in Brisbane, Australia, gets today, Americans and Europeans see tomorrow and want the day after.

These days, for Customers who have the money or who can access the credit, the world is theirs. Now the Customer can really be king. Not like that limp attempt a few made at it the last time. This time it's for real. We've already seen, in the last five years, the 'ante' rising; first, we had Customer satisfaction, then Customer delight (or other similar names), and now we're striving for what you will read about later as 'Customer superformance'. A permanent, dynamic, unceasing desire to exceed Customer expectations with every transaction or contact. Every time a WOW. A veritable field of miracles waiting to be harvested.

How can you change the way you sell?

Given the choice – and they will be – no Customer in his right mind would want to deal with a salesperson driven by quantity objectives. Customers already know that, so often, quantity objectives work against quality objectives. It is only those who sell to them who fail to do anything positive about this dichotomy.

Look at the classic high-commission businesses and the reputation they have: double-glazing or replacement windows, timeshare, perhaps even office equipment. There are many more, including, sadly (despite a maze of absurd but entirely necessary self-regulation), some of the financial services. I so often listen to insurance people bemoaning the tight corset of bureaucratic legislation in Europe and

Australasia – called, for example, Compliance and Disclosure in Britain – that is forced upon them. 'No other business has so explicitly to tell Customers how much their charges are and how much commission the salespeople are getting,' they say.

Don't they realize they brought it on themselves by failing to respond to consumers' demands? Didn't they constantly respond only to their own greed? Insurance, it seems to me, is about protection. The psychology that believes that I would want to deal with or, more importantly, to remain long and spend more with, someone who is aggressive (or threatening) is preposterous. It actually forces Customers to review their choice at the very next purchase, precisely because Mr Hard Sell managed to intimidate them into it the first time. No miracles there.

The basic premise of this book has two dimensions. The first is that, for businesses, quantity objectives generally work against quality objectives. The second dimension is that the reverse is not true. Quality objectives can most definitely work for quantity objectives. This is why, when you get the quality right for Customers, you sell your wares and make profits in far greater quantity.

However, let us stay with the first dimension: quantity objectives generally work against quality. This notion is going to cause complete upheaval in selling and advertising, let alone the whole spectrum of marketing and marketing services for the quality-driven age. This will be the age not just of product excellence, or of cost excellence, but mostly of service excellence. In other words, delivery of the corporate promise.

Consider it. For 40 years the once noble art of selling tarnished itself by responding to the mindless call for more orders. It has become obsessed with 'pile it high, sell it cheap'. You may remember those words as the immortal utterings of Jack Cohen, founder of the British supermarket chain Tesco; this is a company that is now proud to boast about being the greenest, cleanest, most Customer-attentive supermarket chain in the UK. Now they sell quality. Or at least they think they do.

Shock! Horror! It's the future

The future will cause many deep shocks. The pressure put upon business people by quantity objectives has caused many heart attacks. The pressure put upon businesses by quality objectives will cause a new phenomenon – the 'corporate coronary'. It happens as a result of a business trying hard to keep up with the global levels of Customer demand; often, it will quite literally fall to the ground dead. Out of funds, out of time, out of energy; exhausted and exasperated.

With this book you will learn how to avoid such a corporate heart attack yourself – or perhaps how to avoid being the trapped and tragic victim, an employee of a stricken company.

Everyone is talking about change; indeed, everyone is writing about change. I am going to be no exception. For the quite remarkable fact is that few have yet started to explain or describe the changes that will take place in selling, advertising, marketing and servicing Customers. There are a few ex-direct marketers, or information and database manipulators, who have picked up the flag and talk of one-to-one marketing, or, as I call it, 'Individualization'. However, I haven't found anyone yet who has taken a real look at how this affects your whole business. Most still discuss these so-called new concepts as if they are going to take place only in a marketing or a sales department.

No one, to my knowledge, has produced any serious evidence or advice as to how those changes that have already been predicted will affect the people involved. Yet, I maintain, that now even the companies must themselves change to deliver quality in all aspects of marketing – advertising, selling, promotions, public relations, and all the other facets of their communications and their processes of persuasion. And that must include service and operations too. When the need to change is seen, these questions must be asked: how can you change the way you sell? How must you change the way you deliver service to Customers? How can you create your own miracles?

Is it back to the drawing board?

Yes and no. For many sales, marketing and service people, in the way that they operate, it is indeed back to the drawing board. But, as in so many other facts of business life, it is first of all a question of back to the board*room*. Quality, as has already been demonstrated by the other founding fathers of the movement, is a boardroom matter. Perhaps, now that it has reached into and beyond the marketing zone, it has actually become a matter even for shareholders. For it often requires mountains of courage and a massive financial investment. And often an enormous leap of faith. As I write that, I am aware of just how many project teams of which I have been a member, or with whom I have acted as a consultant, have found themselves lacking numbers. Yes, an outcome feels right, and appeals intensely to the gut, but has little by way of hard numbers upon which a board can make a decision.

One particular project involving an insurance business comes to mind. The likely costs of their set of miracles looked to be around £19 million. It involved a total restructure, fairly massive re-engineering, a complete new corporate culture and management style and, later, was to involve a 'Customer delight' programme, which then added a further £12.5 million's worth of miracles to the total cost. All this was finally accepted both by the board and by the group board without any real end-game numbers to measure the success of the projects.

We shall look at this aspect – the numbers, or lack of them, and the leap of faith – in more detail again. My point is that it cannot be some short campaign. It's no good putting it on the 'topics for training' for a month or two. There are no miracles there.

This is not merely a question of how well you survive the next 40 years, it is *whether* you will survive to see the next 40. It has taken 40 years for the pendulum to swing in the quantity direction. In my view, it is quite likely that the quality direction swing could last almost as long.

So who has to change? And how?

The kind of changes we are talking about – especially the future of sales, marketing and service – will be looked at in this book from many standpoints. Take the salesman. (Incidentally, I use the term 'salesman' and other similar words throughout this book in a non-sexist, genderless sense, as a generic term. You may also note that the words 'Customer' or 'Client' are always spelt with a capital 'C'. This is not to confound the typesetters, but a personal quirk! I always encourage my Clients to adopt the same discipline throughout their business – this simple idiosyncrasy constantly serves, every time the words are used, to remind us that, commercially, there is nobody to be held in higher esteem.) How should the salesman, he or she, actually sell in the future? How will management change the environment, conditions and terms under which sales employees work in order to engender, measure and reward quality? How will the company restructure its sales and marketing teams to deliver quality, if restructure they must?

We will examine the view that selling is not about a single sale. Nor even is it about a series of sales. Miracles are born of 'Success through Excess'. It is about success through exceeding expectations – Customer superformance. This is the achievement of sales success through delivery of active, as opposed to passive, satisfaction to the Customer. The WOW Factor. We will look at the Customer loyalty issue and see why so many are missing the point, settling for fidelity rather than loyalty.

There is to some degree also a matter of perspective. When the seller and the buyer have different perspectives, their starting points in negotiation are on opposite sides of the fence. When they are both on the same side, trust grows, loyalty abounds and success is a natural result. A miracle has taken place.

So where are we now?

Where exactly are we now? What stage have communications reached – whether for advertising, selling, Customer recruitment, retention or repair?

There is a convenient 'yardstick' in observing the evolution process of direct marketing. Because direct marketing relies so much on other aspects – computers, machinery, printing processes, all the creative tasks of photography, typesetting, and so forth – it's an interesting and valid example.

In the 1950s, soap coupons worth just a few pence were distributed the length and breadth of Britain by direct mail. These days, no one would even think about it. They would use house-to-house distribution for that task and probably harness one of the increasingly sophisticated targeting systems to select the audience that most carefully matched the known profile of their Customer. Using addressed, stamped direct mail would no longer be considered viable, effective, or worthwhile simply to disseminate low-value soap coupons.

In the 1950s, advertisers would happily send out a mailing of 250,000, in which each and every mailing package was identical, distinguished only by the name on the outside of the envelope. By the 1960s, that same organizer of the 250,000 mailing was looking at new capabilities. Increased knowledge about the market, increased mechanization of mailing lists, increased recognition of the importance of market sectors, and increased postage had combined to make greater cost-effectiveness both possible and necessary. One way to achieve this was to break down the market into groups; for the sake of the rest of this example, let us imagine that they are all the same size.

So a company would now organize perhaps 25 different mailings of 10,000 within the total of 250,000. Equally, the next decade held new opportunities. By the 1970s, we were drawing well into the age of computerization. People across the world were being exhorted to put their lists on to computer.

I remember how we used to balance out the number of times the list would be used against its size. How we would calculate the likelihood and number of selections that might be required to help a Client decide between staying on a manual system, or choosing the mechanical addressing systems, or the infant but capable computer, complete with all its teething problems. Problems or not, the advantages far outweighed the disadvantages and so we moved into the next phase.

Now our 250,000 mailing could consist of 1,000 different mailings of 250 like packages. This was the beginning of the Age of Personalization, which was only finally to be unseated and replaced towards the end of the 1980s. During the 1980s, we saw the blossoming of the laser printer. In those few years, that printer changed from a rather unreliable $500,000 ten-metre box to a desktop at less than $5,000, with many cheaper still. Moreover, as the direct marketing industry grew, aligning itself alongside the computer industry, so the software market became more sophisticated.

The growth in direct mail also warranted research and development in other production technologies. Now, there is mail-enclosing machinery, which will take a whole range of different leaflets, brochures and other enclosures and, based on the letter being sent, enclose the relevant materials with each letter.

You can understand why I explain to audiences that we have transcended the Age of Personalization and arrived at the Age of Individualization. This is the age when we need to make miracles happen! For there is no reason why each person in the mailing should not today receive an offer, proposition, message, or whatever, which is entirely individual to them, cognizant of their own individual circumstances, and recognizing all the multiple facets of their particular relationship with the advertiser.

Now, that original mailing in fact comprises 250,000 completely individual mailings. But this is not the only evidence of the Age of Individualization. For this is also the time when, while the motor trade in Germany still asks three months to take the order for your precise specification of car and then deliver it to you, in Japan, you can have your own individualized car in just a few days. It's a miracle! For the moment.

In the USA, one refrigerator manufacturer, I'm told, asks you these questions before supplying you with *your* equipment. After all, who else would want it?

- How big is the gap you wish to fill?
- Describe your family's eating and drinking habits. Particularly tell us about cooled drinks, salads and fresh foods, and frozen foods.
- Please send examples of your kitchen decor. Any exterior colour can be matched, and toning shelf and interior materials will be offered before building.
- Please advise which of the following you would like built in to your unit: stereo radio/cassette/CD player; black and white or colour TV; video.

Reading the last question, you might decide they've gone too far. After all, designing a unit which reflects the family's consumption and actual storage needs is one thing; trying to turn the fridge into an entertainment centre is something else. Not so, says the company. Their research shows that almost 70 per cent of free-standing equipment ends up with a radio, CD, TV or tape player on top of it. All they do is organize your kitchen for you as an individual or individual family. Miraculous stuff, eh?

Levi's jeans can now be bought over the Internet. The jeans are, in effect, tailor-made. You simply enter your measurements, choose the style you want and they're made for you. Over 1.5 million choices are possible. It's called 'mass-customization'.

As time passes you will see the phenomenon of individualization grow larger. It's inspired not just by the producer's ability to harness design and manufacturing technology, and to deliver such products, but also by the consumer's need to differentiate himself and his belongings from an increasingly uniform and de-humanized world.

In contrast, I was chatting to another of the grey panthers of the global direct marketing scene a while back. He had sold his shareholding in his agency and retired with a very nice sum. The vast majority of his money had been wisely invested but he, for some personal reason, had decided to keep about £100,000 on deposit at his bank where he kept his normal banking facility. This was the same bank that had seen these happy sums of money go through on their way to being invested. On the morning of our call, he had received a heavily personalized mailing offering him a £5,000 unsecured loan!

The fact is that many people are talking about individualization of their marketing, but few have actually got anywhere near it. Many are still satisfied with the relatively prehistoric ways of 30 years ago. Yet, whether we like it or not, here we are in the Age of Individualization. And that is, in many ways, our starting point. Glance around you now.

Find where you and your business are. Remember it well, because the future has some difficult and frightening times in store – times of uncertainty and high risk.

You will remember these present times for the ease with which you could do business, the ease with which you could make money…and the ease with which you could satisfy your Customers. Times will change beyond all recognition.

Far be it for me to put the fear of God into you about the future, but that's exactly what I think might need to happen. I, and many others before me, have pointed to change being the cause of this fear. Not just change itself, but its rate and frequency and scope.

A definition of change might be 'making or becoming different', but this is not quite what I mean. I would like to build in far greater emphasis on the future inconsistency and unreliability of the status quo. The status quo should no longer be seen as cosy. It will be the status quo for a decreasing amount of time. You're going to need one miracle after another.

This means in turn that things you used to rely on – product life-cycles, a competitive edge, Customer satisfaction, material sources, prices and suppliers, and so on – many of these will become unreliable and untrustworthy in the next decade.

In such circumstances you must look to make yourself stronger, more resilient. I have two suggestions for this. The first lies in your business process; the second in the quality of what you use marketing to create. Specifically, I am referring to your quality objectives. For one aspect of the quantity/quality discussion we have not considered is this: quantity only builds immediate sales; quality builds friends. Friends, in the long term, build greater quantity, which yields the miracles.

What factors will most affect a Customer-driven business in the future?

When we examine the factors that will most affect business in the future, we discover some rather predictable old friends – such as the economy – as well as some new ones. Indeed, the whole thing is a bit of a jigsaw. And it may only be when all but the very last few pieces are in place that you will start to resolve your own uncertainties and make decisions about your future.

I'm sure you'll find great comfort in all you read in this book, although a great deal of the contents may challenge you, your thinking and your present practices. In which case, I will have had my say and you will have had value. For this is the true purpose of this book: to change things for the better, for the Customer. In other words, for you.

How much you agree, how much you accept, how much you think about, how much you change is, of course, ultimately and eternally your decision. You may not entirely enjoy what you read. Several times after presentations, I have sat chatting to ('comforting' might be a better word) participants who have spent one or two days working on what I call their Customer gap. That's to say examining the way they want to be treated as Customers and the way they choose or are instructed to treat their Customers. Such gaps are often wide and the desired outcome of these sessions is to look at how that gap can be closed. Frequently there is fallout!

On the positive side, we get the Eureka types – people who leave feeling that they have seen the light. They know what they want to do, know how they want to go about it and can't wait to get back to work the next day and get started. On the negative side, we get the trapped or the powerless. Some of these people feel incredibly frustrated. Some are downright angry. They know what they should do, understand the deep sense and 'rightness' of it, but know also that there is no way their company or their bosses will even contemplate it.

New methods for you, new directions for your business

All around the world, I come face to face with front-line teams or team members, and their immediate managers, sensing and embracing their new ability to think and make a difference. However, these people still come up against enormous opposition from senior managers, who are saying all the right things, but having terrible problems letting go of their power and their old ways of command and control.

Today – and when I describe this I always picture the biblical waters coming back together after Moses and the children of Israel had passed through – the old energy flow from senior management is still coming from one direction while from the other comes this enormous rush of excitement, commitment and fulfilment. The result is a mind-numbing clash of cultures and methods – the waters coming together – which is causing upset and anger, like an incredibly disruptive backwash.

As you move your business forward to becoming Customer-driven, these matters must command your attention. If they are to be successful, and untap so much of their future potential, Customer-focused organizations need these new structures, styles and cultures. It is precisely these factors that release the treasure chest of human talent that will enable the organizations to compete more and more effectively. This is just more evidence that the silo-style boundaries of the past are tumbling all around us with increasing speed. We cannot and must not see marketing, sales, advertising or Customer service in terms of those old-fashioned boundaries of the past. They are integrating and embedding themselves deep into the heart of every aspect, every function, every activity of business.

Lastly, just before we come to the end of this first chapter, I'd like to point something out. It might seem obvious, but I'll say it none the less. Don't look for the switch. There isn't one. You can't turn a miracle on. There is nothing anybody can or will flick to change the environment from product-driven to Customer-driven. It is truly a pendulum; possibly even a 40-year pendulum. Some people will do some of the things you are going to read about. Some will not. Some will do all of them. Some none. Some will do them tomorrow. Some in five years' time. The only thing you need to know about this pendulum is that it is relentless; in fact, it is unstoppable.

A revolution is under way. Marketing, sales, advertising and service people cannot escape this revolution. The Customers have taken control. They can take their business anywhere. The survivors, the winners, will be those who master the new techniques and learn the ways of a Customer-driven business and, therefore, what has to come next. Let's call them the miracle makers. They have discovered that it's all about Customers.

The major points of this chapter relating to the marketing environment and how it affects the business are:

- The bigger a business gets, the harder it becomes to respond to Customers and to manage Customer relationships.
- Given the choice, Customers prefer not to deal with a salesperson driven by quantity objectives. Customers know that quantity objectives work against quality objectives.
- We have arrived at the Age of Individualization. This relates to products and services, not just the media used to sell them.
- Quantity builds immediate sales. Quality builds friends for your business. Those friends build the long-term quantity that yields the miracles.

2

Marketing and sales: new dimensions, new objectives, new thinking

Customer-driven marketing – the notion of driving a business by Customer issues – is different from product-driven marketing. It's harder, for a start. It requires greater degrees of professionalism, better use of intelligence, more understanding, more information and a different culture.

Providing the information is perhaps the easiest part of all of these – databases to the rescue! However, professionalism, intelligence, understanding and culture require not only that we do our job better, but that we do a better job. In other words, the new Customer-driven ethos must attach both to what we do, and to the way that we do it. This means it is essential that we build quality through defined objectives in both those areas. Conventional management techniques already provide us with the means to achieve these ends. Although, the other day, I did find myself in a project definition meeting that was addressing radical product change for a financial services Client. 'Why', I wondered, 'do we set about instigating or developing change in the same old way?' It's a question I haven't satisfactorily answered for myself yet!

However, before we go any further, let me place a view before you about the scope and influence of marketing in a Customer-driven business.

Marketing is a four-way process

To achieve its full effective power, and to provide you with its full benefit, I believe marketing must be a four-way process. Although I believe the needs for marketing towards your Customers and prospects (forward external marketing) are well accepted, I'm not sure the other three dimensions are. These are: marketing to your own colleagues (internal marketing); to your suppliers and sub-contractors (reverse external marketing); and then to your shareholders (support marketing).

Let's examine this notion a little further.

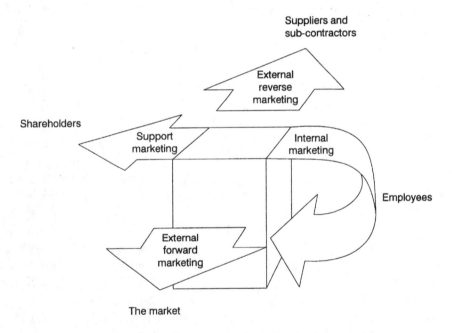

Figure 2.1 The four-way marketing model

Internal marketing – to your own staff

For some years now I have been offering a high-level marketing strategy course for directors and other senior people who are involved in longer-term corporate strategy. On this course we discuss the four dimensions of marketing. When we come to discuss internal marketing, lots of hands have gone up over the years to affirm, 'Yes, we do this.' The notion is not new. However, after probing a little further, we find out that their view of internal marketing often has very limited scope and involves communicating with the salespeople, the Customer service people or the branches or outlets who deal with Customers. It is deemed to be simply about keeping them up to date or involved with the latest marketing activities. This is barely sufficient. And not at all about getting buy-in from the business and support for what marketing is trying to do.

Why is this so important? It's vital because a Customer-driven business lives and breathes commitment and passion. Therefore, it needs to be staffed by teams of people who are motivated, understand the bigger picture and who know their part in it – from the financial director to the person on the switchboard, from the guys in Accounts to the techies in IT.

Getting the whole business behind a Customer-driven mission, vision and values is the job of the business leader. The marketing team is a natural choice as his or her support unit, thus acting as guardians of both function and culture. It is important that the team remembers to market marketing. Financial directors, for example, have to understand the value of the brand and why Customer loyalty is important both financially and otherwise – as well as simple information such as sales figures, which says nothing about how well the business is really doing. In Personnel or HR, do they know why we want high-quality people, do they appreciate the importance we place on front-line activity? Can they train to the quality we need? Can they show empowered people how to take responsibility?

Reverse external marketing – to your suppliers

Reverse external marketing is sadly still born of, and generally reserved for, times of scarce or limited resources, when it is used to ensure continuity of supply and, as far as possible, maintenance of price. I remember first seeing reverse external marketing used tactically during the three-day weeks and power rationing caused by the industrial disputes in Britain in the 1970s. Colt, a major heating and ventilating equipment manufacturer, simply switched its whole marketing effort into reverse thrust and, as a result, surprised both its market and its competitors by making optimum use of its own limited production times. Not only was its resource planning careful, but somehow it also always seemed to have the wherewithal to manufacture while the others were making more excuses than equipment.

A while ago I was whisked off to Västerås in Sweden to address an audience of about 800 for ABB. It was the second convention the company had held for a fascinating group of people. It was putting its suppliers together with its own teams and their Clients. It represented a genuine partnership approach, in which all had been able to overcome the conventional fear about 'giving away' their sources and secrets. Instead, ABB had stood the whole thing on its head and, in a spirit of complete openness and partnership, was encouraging a full team mentality to brainstorming and problem solving. I wish I saw such genuine, trusting, 'everyone wins' approaches to building lasting Customer relationships more frequently. I also greatly admire the confidence the company has in the value of its own skills, and the trust it builds in both its Clients and suppliers.

The moral of these examples is that supplier relations are crucial to delivery of the Customer promise and, as such, in my view, merit planned strategic marketing. In becoming a Customer-driven business your business efficiency has to increase. Trying to do this without the full support of your suppliers will severely limit your chances. I often think this is like planes re-fuelling in flight. If one increased its speed and the other didn't, not a lot of fuel would get through! You and your suppliers have to be flying at the same speed.

Talk to external suppliers and to others in the chain. Involve everyone, gain their commitment and support – their commitment will build as you work at the problems and you share the responsibilities and benefits together.

You may feel that running this kind of marketing continuously, when I have referred to it as being excellent in times of resource shortage or threat, may be a little extreme. That depends on your resources and your suppliers – and I would propose that the ABB experience suggests otherwise. But the fact that I am suggesting *all* corporations should provide for external reverse marketing in their total marketing effort serves to underline the seriousness of my warning in relation to change, and to the extent and suddenness with which it will strike.

Support marketing

I often refer to shareholders as the insiders outside. I know that for many years some corporations have been offering fidelity 'bonuses' and other perks to retain shareholders. This is not what I mean by 'support marketing'. I have no proof, but I suspect that these kinds of loyalty or fidelity schemes suffer the same inherent flaws as Customer loyalty schemes, which ultimately rely on bribery. They don't build anything like as much loyalty as businesses hope because the only human appeal is basically to greed.

I am cognizant here of the increasing number of institutional shareholders, such as US mutual funds and what the British call unit trusts. These shareholders are basically there to provide a return of capital growth or dividends for their own Customers or investors. 'Long term' is not the watchword of such people and, when businesses are seeking to undergo a period of change or transformation, which many will associate with risk, these kinds of shareholder need careful management and sensitive communication.

Relationships not transactions

To a great extent quantity objectives have forced businesses to concentrate on trying to create a number of transactions. The new desire is to establish the requisite number of Customer relationships that will in turn create sales. Thus, if your business is to become Customer-driven, you will have to understand that your work must create the means for such relationships to grow and prosper and that transactions will result. Understanding how this affects your business is important. Look at the locations, the atmosphere, the staff, the facilities and the circumstances in which your Customers will find themselves and question whether you have created a forum for transactions or relationships. Also, take a look at the processes and techniques you use. For example how do you use sales promotion? The more aggressive the techniques used in generating new Customer transactions, the less substance the business generated has for the future. Let's consider this along with some other interesting facts...

What makes advertising work?

While considering the new objectives for marketing a Customer-driven business, let us not become totally obsessed with quality. Let's think about quantity too. In direct marketing, the media and style of so many campaigns enables you to test quite scientifically, and indeed quite economically, all manner of variations to see which perform best.

One particularly interesting set of statistics, which I use as a discussion point in many conferences, was gathered by a leading international direct marketing agency through a most comprehensive analysis. They were trying to establish which factors most affected response rates, and in what proportions. Here are their findings:

FACTORS AFFECTING RESPONSE
Response device – 20 per cent
Creativity – 35 per cent
Timing – 100 per cent
The Offer – 200 per cent
The List – 500 per cent

I understand these figures were gained by measuring the best and worst situations. Thus, for example, if a mailing with a badly conceived reply device would pull an index of 100, and a mailing that was identical but with a good device 120, the result was a response uplift of 20 per cent. The results were taken from many, many efforts, and the agency concerned was convinced of the validity of the results. To be clear about their findings, the first figure suggests that you will get a response improvement of typically 20 per cent (ie from, say, 2 per cent to 2.4 per cent) simply by thoughtful and informed attention to detail on the reply card or response device you are using. From experience, I know this to be so; and those in the financial services or insurance fields, in which applications can tend to be quite long and complex, will also know this to be the case.

The next statistic, however, is something of a poser. Can it really be true that the total difference between indifferent and stunning creativity should be just 35 per cent? Whenever I discuss this with creative teams they either take umbrage, or just don't believe the figure. It does take a little while for creative sensitivities to work it through. It is also interesting that, according to these statistics, correct timing is almost exactly three times more important than the creative work. Perhaps many salespeople will find that one easy to relate to. Yet the offer or proposition is a remarkable six times more powerful at making the advertising effective than the creative contribution. To be fair, especially in the direct marketing context, many would argue that the two are inextricably woven together. However, when you think of the number of advertisements that carry a message but don't make a proposition or offer, it is easy to see how underrated this simple concept is.

The last figure is really very interesting; it suggests that finding the right audience for your ad is two and a half times more effective than the proposition, five times more critical than timing, and an astounding 15 times more important than the creativity.

This surely must question the current method of choosing an ad agency and the enormous priority given to creative skills in the selection process. On the face of it, here we see the relevance of abilities in the creative process reduced to a relative also-ran.

How do you choose your agency?

Rather than keep fellow proponents of the creative discipline in misery, let me say straight away that there's more to the figures than meets the eye!

Before I burst the balloon, let us ponder a while on what I consider to be a most significant thinking point here. When pitching for business, agencies are rarely asked to give more than a cursory rundown of their media or strategic or planning skills. This is probably because it's the most fun and, to many, the most interesting, absorbing and entertaining; creativity rules! So, in case the following should be construed as a dash to the rescue of creativity, may I also make the plea for true weighting to be given to the other skills? Important as creative is, it is certainly not all-important.

Creativity works to more than the sale

The catch in the figures is that they relate, in direct marketing terms, to what actually affects the response – and the response alone. They place no value at all on the pure advertising effect of the campaigns. Since most direct marketing, and certainly most classical advertising, has an effect on brand and corporate values, which is, of course, largely to the credit of the creativity, we must generally give it a better rating than 35 per cent. However, I feel obliged to say that, in my experience, creativity is none the less one of the most over-priced and wasteful areas of the marketing world and needs a great deal of tightening up.

Raymond Rubicam, co-founder of Young and Rubicam, and one of the forefathers of the international agency scene, once put it most succinctly: 'The object of advertising is to sell goods. It has no other justification worth mentioning.' That statement, although made many years ago, effectively remains true; however, with the increased value that Customer-driven marketing places on brand and corporate strength and loyalty building, we will once again see greater strategic and tactical emphasis placed upon these aspects of marketing.

A new power for corporate image

As the marketing mix reshuffles itself to cope with the future, so each of its disciplines is claiming that they have an increased role in the future. Sales promotion is a fine example, where the practitioners are making all manner of new claims for their trade. They are effectively digging themselves into an entrenched position, which has far more to do with the old ways of exploitation selling than it has to do with satisfaction marketing. However, I know that there are some among their ranks who can and will make this change; and they will reap the rewards they deserve.

I think the only mistake in listening to the voices of the various marketing disciplines would be to take any strategic notice of them. One of those voices can be heard crying out that it shall have increasing prominence – and it is right. It is the voice of the corporate identity, or as I often refer to it, 'the brand behind the brand'.

Boston Consulting was called in by Royal Insurance in the UK. The CEO at that time was Peter Duerden, a man who gave me one of my most frequently used and favourite quotes: 'A key characteristic of successful businesses is their ability to respond to changes in their marketplace before there is any widely held perception of the need to do so.'

Royal Insurance (UK) Ltd – which has since become Royal Sun Alliance – was a wholly owned subsidiary of Royal Insurance plc, the parent holding company of one of the world's largest insurance groups, operating in over 80 countries. Peter Duerden was to lead the company through a sustained strategy of change. Royal reviewed Clients' needs within each of its principle channels of business. The conclusion was that it had to change the organization itself as well as many of its decision-making processes. Dubbing the project 'Channel Focus', Royal had realized that, if its different Clients across its different distribution channels (brokers, agents and financial service intermediaries) had different expectations of the company, it was counter-productive to try to force them all into the same response, delivery and service mechanisms.

Furthermore – sharing great courage and insight in an industry not overburdened with such qualities – Royal set about devolving the decision-making authority in relation to the vast majority of its day-to-day business operations. This authority was passed down to the staff closest to its Clients – in its branches – requiring a new structure, with highly skilled insurance people at branch level.

These changes took some three years to complete and demonstrated that to deliver quality through to Customers many changes must take place outside the traditional remit of marketing. As an observer, I found two factors interesting about the Royal case. In many ways it could be classified as a textbook example in changing direction: a prime example of a huge company doing its utmost to change from one of those faceless self-perpetuating, self-obsessed monsters that manipulate markets to their own ends, to a new leaner, keener, versatile and energetic group of Client-oriented units that live and breathe Customer needs. My first point is that, although these benefits would in time supposedly benefit the end-Customer – the policyholder – in all their re-shaping and re-thinking, Royal seems to have started in the middle, centring all its changes on the intermediary Clients, such as brokers and agents. The assumption here is that the benefits would reach the policyholder in the end.

Second, I found it strange that this 'revolution' took place in just the one Royal group company. A Customer of Royal may have dealt with Royal Insurance for his or her general business (such as household or motor insurance), and with Royal Life for life, savings and pensions products. I suspect that, to most policyholders, 'Royal' was the name they remembered. They probably did not appreciate that there was a difference between Royal Life and Royal Insurance. Surely for the average Customer or prospect, the brand they would remember would be the one word of the company name – Royal.

Yet, if the change programme was to be in any way successful, it would create a real difference between Royal Insurance and its sibling companies. This vast cultural difference could only serve to confuse Customers, who could understandably expect some similarity in methods, systems and services. The more the changes at Royal Insurance became effective, the more significant the problem could have become, as the gap between them increasingly deeply confused Customers.

At chemical multi-national ICI, the brand behind the brand also became an issue. In a totally different market from Royal, ICI managers have had to consider the total needs of some of their Customers. This often stretches beyond the conventional product disciplines that are recognized by ICI. After all, a Customer that buys fertilizers on the one hand, and plastics for packaging on the other, sees itself not as two separate Customers of ICI, but as one. Only ICI separates its needs, and it does so in order to meet ICI structures.

This has led ICI to look at Customers' total industry requirements. Yet individual companies or operating divisions within groups can often be quite competitive and jealously guard their information and contacts. Such petty insecurities may not exist within ICI, but I have often seen the most outrageous non-cooperation between group members. ICI has said that it feels the answer might be in putting together its businesses in structures aligned to the marketplace; my view is that the design of corporate structure starts with Customers and works back. My guess is that ICI's analysis is correct, provided that:

- the business groups can quickly assimilate sufficient expertise in its new specialization and convince its market of the benefits;
- provision is made for the forwarding of the overall corporate strategy and culture; and
- a network for information and communication is created between the market-aligned fragments.

One tendency with market-aligned fragments is for an overflow of commitment to its market sector. This in turn leads each to see its resource demands as the highest priority. When the correct communication, training and information networks are in place, a much better balance between corporate direction and strategy and market sector obsession is achieved.

Brand loyalty needs a strong corporate attachment too

The hard fact is that we face an epoch when there is a convergence of factors over the extent to which an organization's failure to address its corporate image and position will seriously damage its health. The factors include parity products, both better and more similar; and a consumer that is more informed, more vocal, more sophisticated, more demanding and more willing to vote with his or her cash.

Murray Raphael, a valued friend as well as the 'king' of US supermarket marketing, once reminded me that people often bestow human qualities on the companies with which they deal. 'Just listen to the way they describe them,' he explained. 'They say they're a mean outfit. Or pretty generous types. Or friendly. Or stand-offish. These are not corporate qualities, these are the qualities or failings of another human being.' He's right! And so, in a way, it is fair to suggest that a corporate identity is an expression of corporate personality.

Everything a company does, the way it acts, the opinions it expresses, the people it hires, as well as the way it treats its Customers, is seen to a lesser or greater degree as an expression of that personality. Thus, the identity can be used quite powerfully to join with, differentiate from, or simply endorse a chosen position. I am suggesting for the future that, as products become more similar, so the corporate identity should support and enhance the role of the brands. It can help to provide further competitive differentiation. Naturally, the methods used to do this will vary depending on which of the three classic identities the business has adopted. These are:

- the Monolith – an organization that revolves its whole style around one strong core name and visual presentation, such as IBM and BMW.
- the Patron – this company operates through a series of brands, which often have no logical relationship to each other or to the organization. Often the different brands have been added through acquisition or merger. Nestlé and Proctor & Gamble are examples.
- the Umbrella – a cluster organization, which endorses or sponsors multiple activities, such as General Motors and, to some extent, Virgin. Richard Branson, of course, takes it one step further. Is he a man or a brand? Perhaps his family dropped a 'd' somewhere along the way!

Stern words

Northwestern University (Evanston, Illinois, USA) has a distinguished record in leading-edge thinking and teaching in marketing; two very distinguished professors have played a huge part in creating that reputation. One of those professors is Phil Kotler, a man whose work of some 20 years ago is now beginning to look almost prophetic. (He shares this distinction with another prophet, Ted Levett.) The second professor is Louis Stern. Kotler's 'From Sales Obsession to Marketing Effectiveness', published in the 'Harvard Business Review', suggests that 'marketing focuses on the needs of the buyer. It is preoccupied with how to generate Customer satisfaction at a profit.' This is theoretically correct. However, since Kotler wrote that in the late 1970s, many years have passed, and the pendulum that I believe he was trying to stop swaying even further towards its quantity climax, continued regardless for a further 20 years. Now, in semi-retirement,

I believe that he will see it on the way back and, thus, will have the pleasure of being right twice.

Like Kotler – indeed, alongside Kotler – Louis Stern has for some years concerned himself with predicting the trends in marketing. His predictions for the first decade of the millennium suggest that the present trend towards the quality or 'softer' issues of sales and marketing – the relationship issues, that is – will continue. For example, he feels that, whereas the 1990s proved to be a time of customizing and repositioning products to fit the needs of niche markets, the following decade will be a time of streamlining by removing stress from the acquisition and consumption processes; retaining and defending Customers from competitors; and searching for innovations by studying lead Customers.

The market orientation of the 1990s will continue to show an increased concern about how companies take their products to market – particularly about what channels to use, and ease of availability.

Stern is convinced that most companies will want to exceed Customers' expectations with every transaction and interaction; they will also concentrate on developing value propositions – this will continue the trend of moving away from price for price's sake, and take into account how Customers feel, as well as the way they act. The prediction is also that corporations will focus much more on sales growth, but in a much more strategic fashion. That's to say, they will more clearly define the precise set of benefits they will deliver to specific target groups of Customers at a price that yields a profit. I think this is a very significant point, since a great number of the companies I visit fail to distinguish, in terms of level of service, who deserves it and who doesn't. I believe firmly that standards of service should be consistent and sacrosanct. Levels of service should vary, set broadly against the value of the Customer and a reasonable perception by that Customer of what service they should expect for their money. This means it is as important to know who not to target, sell to and serve as it is to know who should be targeted. There is no point in paying out to get Customers who will not be profitable or whose expectations you are not able to meet or exceed.

Stern further suggests that companies must concentrate on providing packages, bundled together into turnkey solutions. Using databases developed in the 1990s, businesses will begin to focus on segments of one. I agree that this is a goal and that some companies may reach it. I also believe that, for many marketers, it should remain a goal or a principle. In reality, we may not yet have developed the technology, the service elements, and the ability to create anything other than commodities out of certain simple and vital necessities of life. These may always be sold on price in certain arenas and on availability or convenience at other times or in other places.

Within a few years, six-sigma standards – in other words, essentially perfect ones – will be the norm and the Customer expectancy. Businesses will appreciate that they must invest in intellectual property (software more than hardware!); that to survive they must transform from being fixed cost businesses to variable cost businesses; and that they must develop into modular or sometimes virtual organizations.

Louis Stern's valuable insights for the future add fuel to the notion that this book proposes, and endorse the view that you should already have started.

Creating sales that stick

I've always been a great believer in the idea that a first sale is only complete when the second sale is set up. If you feel the same way, you may have experienced a phenomenon that is well accepted in direct marketing, and well known but rather less frequently worried about in selling.

The more promotion you use to close a sale, the higher the incidence of, first, the sale failing to complete as Customers cancel (or, perhaps, gather the courage or self-resolve to withdraw). Second, the more worries, complaints and attempts to retract you get during the 'buyer's remorse' period; and, third, the less likely it is that the Customer will proceed to a second or third sale eventually leading to optimum lifetime values.

On a rather pedantic technical note, it should be said that some direct marketers would argue that a 'flimsy' low-commitment first sale is better than no sale, since it gives the opportunity to create a more solid basis through the ensuing dialogue. This could be generally correct. However, the point to which I would like to draw particular attention is that the logic for the phenomenon also holds a moral. The more manipulated Customers have been to pressure the sale through, the less receptive they are to the second approach. Moreover, companies that adopt heavy or continuous highly promotional methods tend to attract the kind of Customer who responds to them. By definition, these will often be the kind of 'scavengers' who have less loyalty to give and who, therefore, will be more easily moved on by a better offer or bigger discount from anyone else. These people can collect premiums, gifts, and incentives in the way that squirrels gather nuts.

If your business survives on such people and can stand the cost of marketing to them, or can sustain the high level of expensively gained conquest business, then this will not trouble you. You are a 'high-activity marketer'. High-activity marketers use exploitation selling. It is an aggressive process, which bribes, cajoles and tempts the prospect with lots and lots of 'goodies'! The same 'goodies', incidentally, used to tempt the less likely into buying will often be more effectively used as loyalty rewards or benefits.

It is only when high-activity marketers crave miracles that they will start to consider new thinking. Then they will want to understand the costs of not working on Customer loyalty; and it is at that moment that they might take fright. People are always anxious that becoming a Customer-driven business is going to cost them more money. It doesn't. It makes more money. Those who have experienced extra cost have generally been those who have invested in additional service to Clients believing that they've now done what needs to be done. For a Customer-driven business to reap maximum return, it must do things that save money as well as things that cost money. And there are plenty of savings to be made, as we will see in Chapter 5.

Apples don't grow on companies

When you consider how to add quality to your organization's marketing it needs to be appreciated that businesses and apple trees don't have too much in common. Apple trees can regularly produce quantity and quality. Businesses have been obsessed with the delivery of quantity for so long that quality and Customer goals will cause them stress and require much effort and commitment from all concerned. However, the return of Customer objectives to business yields a benefit for the company that will become a real treasure chest of an asset. By using its Customer-driven process across its four dimensions, it engenders stable, durable relationships, which, enhanced by quality products and services, will lock Customers, staff and suppliers together around the corporate core.

When the decision is made to incorporate such objectives, they must be built in on a formal basis, which enables success to be monitored and analysed. Although many of these objectives will be philosophical and cultural, it is still essential that they can be managed and measured. We need to ensure we can see how well we're doing in our quest for the business. The quest? It's all about Customers.

In this chapter, we have considered the following:

- A business with a Customer-driven culture finds life much harder than a conventional quantity-driven business with a transaction marketing culture. It seeks greater professionalism, intelligence and understanding of the Customer and information. Of these, information may prove the easiest, using database solutions.
- Marketing has four dimensions: forward external – to your Customers; internal – to your own staff; external reverse – to suppliers; and support marketing – to shareholders.
- In the battle to differentiate choices in a market of increasingly similar products, corporate identity will play an increasing part as a 'brand behind the brand'.
- Professor Louis Stern's predictions for the mix of strategies that corporations must adopt if they are to survive and thrive in the next decade support the whole notion of the Customer-driven business, and there is no sign of any swing or change in this.
- Marketers must create forums that cultivate relationships rather than simply generate transactions. In this respect, businesses will need to adjust their objectives to require less promotion and build a more solid Customer base. A business that uses exploitation processes attracts a less loyal type of Customer who is more easily tempted away by others. Quality marketers enjoy longer-lasting, more profitable, more satisfying relationships with their Customers.

3

What will Customers want next?

There seem to be hordes of people who involve themselves in Customer care tactics and very few involved in the strategy. This is a very great shame. And no miracles there! Customer care – if it is to provide anything like the levels required for a relationship-centred Customer-driven business – should not be thought of as a tactic. It has to be considered strategically and systematically.

So many of the companies I meet talk passionately about Customer care (as they often do, incidentally, about quality), and then treat it as some kind of occasional or spasmodic campaign. Displaying a certificate in reception celebrating the person in the organization who did something outstanding for a Customer last month is a campaign. Expecting *all* your employees routinely to do something outstanding for a Customer every month, every week or every day suggests that you've got a strategy in place.

And when it goes right...

I rang a restaurant that used to be a regular haunt, but that I hadn't visited for over ten years. Paul, the owner, answered the phone and, as soon as I announced myself, more than ten years dissolved as if they had never been. We had some catching-up time and then I told Paul that I would like a table for six the following Sunday. 'Sure,' he said, 'would you like your usual table?' Not bad after more than a decade!

Maybe you have a favourite good service story, or perhaps know a place where you always feel special, or even welcome. Perhaps you have places you go where you're recognized and made a fuss of. If you're typical, you'll react by going there regularly, taking your friends and generally giving them a terrific 'word of mouth' testimonial whenever you get the opportunity. I have always described word of mouth as the cheapest, most effective kind of advertising you can buy: the trouble is, of course, you can't buy it. You have to earn it. I maintain, and I know that I am among many who feel this way, that we are going to see all this change radically.

The following research was published by CMT Direct. They had the motor insurance market under their particular microscope and discovered that, based on a sample of 65,000 motorists, 'word of mouth' provided the motor insurance business with more name awareness than television, press and direct mail put together. In fact, 'word of mouth' tops the list at a tad more than 27 per cent. Let this tell you something about what your Customers will do for you – if you get it right!

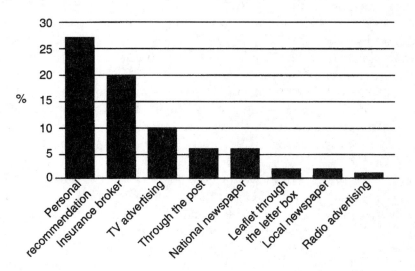

Source: CMT Direct Marketing

Figure 3.1 Word of mouth outscores advertising in creating name awareness for motor insurance – and probably most else as well

Who enjoys their shopping these days?

To get a measure on how sales and marketing people feel about shopping I have made a point during all my Marketing 2000 conferences of asking audiences, 'Hands up. Who enjoys going to the supermarket?' There are some who do. In fact, if I'm honest, I do! I enjoy watching the people and I enjoy casting a professional eye over the marketing and, particularly, the sales promotion that is going on. But do we enjoy the shopping? My show-of-hands research tells me that few people do.

News just in!

The unpopularity of shopping was confirmed as I write this chapter by a survey carried out by GfK GB Research, who interviewed Customers of Sainsbury and Midland Bank. Of the 2,000 women questioned, 38 per cent at banks and 57 per cent at supermarkets declared they 'hate' shopping.

Asked to rate potential annoyances at home or while shopping, on an irritation scale of 1 to 10, shopping proved far more annoying than housework. Ironing rated 5.6 while laundry was deemed therapeutic in comparison, scoring a lowly 3.4. Crowded shops scored 6.4; seeing an item you had already bought at a higher price in a sale rated 7.4 and pushy sales staff 7.5. By retail sector, car dealers led with an unpopularity rating of 61 per cent, closely followed by banks, electrical stores and chemists, all of whom gained black marks for poor Customer service. So much for the myth of 'retail therapy'!

While on assignment I spent some time in the English seaside town of Weymouth in Dorset. The bank I used there had 'streamlined' itself to have perhaps a dozen cashiers or tellers and two personal bankers. I decided to visit during a lunch hour and found myself in a queue of some 30 or more people, waiting like good citizens to have the honour of a cashier's attention for a short spell. It was well organized. If you visited during the lunch hour, half the cashiers were at lunch, so the management team had thoughtfully installed a Q-matic. This ingenious device told you, when you were lucky enough to get to the front, which of the cashiers not at lunch would pass the time of day with you. To celebrate this golden moment it chimed like a slightly demented doorbell.

As I waited with the other Customers, many of whom, like half the cashiers, were on their lunch break, it became quite obvious that the system the management had devised worked extremely well for the bank, but was the subject of some resentment and anger from their Customers. As I got to the front of the queue, I turned to face the long thin line of angry and frustrated people behind me. 'Excuse me,' I said just loudly enough to get most of their attention. 'Why do you put up with this atrocious service?' I thought I'd be a hero, chair-lifted on to the shoulders of the two chaps behind me, and taken on a tour of the premises while the rest of the queue followed chanting the magic plea, 'We shall, we shall soon be served.' It was not to be. Most of them looked at me and prayed they wouldn't find me sitting next to them on the bus home. So to those nice Dorset folk, and to those members of my audiences who don't enjoy shopping, I say again: 'Why do you put up with it?'

The answer lies in the 1960s

What has all this to do with marketing? Not so much as it has to do with the mentality that took over the driving seat of marketing. Banking, it seems, is not an experience you should enjoy, it is something you have to put up with in order to get the facility. Why do supermarket Customers report that shopping is such a joyless impersonal experience? Why are supermarkets surprised by the findings?

The fact is, Customers have been conditioned to accept it as such. I take Britain to task particularly, but I am enough of a traveller to know that the problem is in no way peculiar to the British (although Britain is certainly the worst in Europe).

But it wasn't always like that. I used to have a Grocery Fairy. Most children have a tooth fairy. Me, I had this Grocery Fairy! The tooth fairy visits in the middle of the night and generously exchanges money for your first teeth as they are lost. My Grocery Fairy didn't get any teeth, but, nevertheless, generously donated a box of groceries to my mother every Friday. Miraculously, the Grocery Fairy always seemed to know exactly what we wanted and always called, as regular as clockwork, before mother got me back from school each Friday.

Eventually, I discovered the truth. It wasn't a fairy at all. You've guessed! It was a grocer. The nice man who patted my head whenever I went into his shop with my mother. The man to whom she always spent such a long time chatting about this and that. The grocer.

This was the mid-1950s. Our grocer used to ring up on a Thursday evening to discuss the weather, exchange family news, and ask my mother whether she wanted anything more than 'the usual'. Sometimes she had a list. Sometimes he prompted her. Sad to think it'll never happen like that again...

The return of the Grocery Fairy (with slightly clipped wings)

Here comes one of my favourite miracles. As you will read, it had nothing to do with me. I just wish it had had!

'What do you make of this?' said my fellow diner, waving a credit card-sized piece of plastic under my nose with obvious pride.

'A credit card?', I ventured.

'Nothing so ordinary,' he laughed. 'It's your Customer Visiting Card for my supermarket. A Customer comes in, swipes it, now the store knows they're there.'

'Aha, security!' I tried again.

'Better than that. My store helps them to shop.'

The owner of this particular chain of stores went on to describe his pride and joy. As each Customer enters a store, they swipe in, and the visit is logged. As they arrive at the checkout, a further swipe alerts the computer and, as the checkout operator works through their purchases, the machine logs them and checks them out against previous buying patterns. The computer then reminds them of any purchases they may have forgotten, based on their previous purchasing patterns. The operator keys in the products they decide to take. Next, they are shown a screen full of special offers based on what the system knows they like, what is in stock and on offer.

'My Customers love this service! It's just like they used to get in the old days. If they want any of the offers they tell the cashier, she adds it in. By the time we've packed for them and they're on the way out, their extra goods are waiting at the door, in a box, with their name on. On top of all that wizardry, they get a loyalty value bonus that builds every time they shop here, they get express priority at the checkouts, and free coffee in the coffee shop. Is that good, or is that great?'

'That's great,' I agreed, my mind doing handstands at the information that his database could yield on purchase patterns, cross-brand selling and the opportunities for phone calls just like my mother used to get.

'What's more', he continued, regaining my attention as his enthusiasm bubbled over, 'the database marketing opportunities are incredible. You know, we ring up people who've missed a visit, and offer to drop their goods round! What do you say about that?'

I looked at this happy, happy man. He had found a WOW factor. When you're on to a winner, it's a first and you know you can license it round the world, it's a fabulous feeling. He looked at me, waiting for the mixture of envy, fascination and admiration that the story no doubt always provokes. His expression became puzzled as I, without thinking, turned to him and replied, 'You remind me of a fairy I once had.'

Back home in the UK, I have been a regular, indeed card-carrying, Customer of Tesco. In one town where we lived I got to know Harry, the guy who ran the fish counter, rather well. I didn't eat meat at that time, but I ate a lot of fish. Harry soon realized this, and he also realized that there were many times when my wife and I didn't seem to frequent the store. He asked me why, and I explained that I, and often we, went overseas quite a lot. 'Hey,' asked Harry, 'how about I call you when we have specials? That way you can top up the freezer and save a lot of money. In fact, if you let me know your favourites, I'll keep some by for you even if you're away.' It sounded good to us and, for two years, until we eventually moved, that is exactly what happened. Harry became my fish man. It was only when we broke it to him that we were moving that he admitted that he was 'actually quite relieved!' We were puzzled. It transpired that, in order to call us up on the phone to tell us about the specials, Harry had to get permission every time to phone out. Harry went on to tell us that there was a new manager in and he was deeply suspicious of Harry's phone calls to us! Oh, Harry, you had it right, my friend; they were the short-sighted, crazy ones!

With Tesco we can find a perfect example of pie machines not making pasta (to revert to my earlier analogy). Tesco was one of Europe's first to embark upon what I would call a Customer fidelity programme, and what most of the marketing fraternity would call a Customer loyalty programme – although, sadly, it seems to rely largely on a discount platform. My experience is that bribery does not build loyalty for long. Others can peel people away with bigger, better bribes.

It is important, as Tesco eventually realized, to look beyond such programmes. No one can or should deny Tesco the credit for getting into the number one slot in the UK principally on the back of its points card. However, certainly for the early years, the card enabled nothing more than targeted sales promotion. It was clever and effective targeted sales promotion, but it was sales promotion none the less. To succeed with tangible, sustainable loyalty programmes we have to work in the 'soft issues', as well as the traditional old hard issues. Real loyalty is built in the emotions, even if it is expressed physically by the act of shopping or buying.

You need people people

'People who need people are the luckiest people in the world,' goes the song. And it's absolutely true. If you're looking to create an environment that cultivates relationships, you will have to ensure that you have the right people up front.

It is more necessary than ever to consider each person's ability to relate to people as a criterion in their work, which will, after all, be the business of building and managing relationships. This is not simply the question of smiling, being nice and saying the right thing – although that seems to be hard enough for many businesses. It is a question of understanding the Customer, looking at the longer term, and creating the kind of atmosphere in which trust, loyalty, respect and even affection can develop. The chemistry between the individuals will be more vital the closer and longer the relationship becomes.

Loyal staff breed loyal Customers. And a company that wants to 'superform' needs superstaff. Super employees are not created overnight. They are never super on their first day. If things go right, they improve as time passes. Customers love the experience, the product or service knowledge – and they love to deal with motivated people who admire and are loyal to their employers. Customers take comfort, because it reassures them and endorses their own good feelings, or perhaps makes them see that any bad experience is an exception. And the other thing Customers love is consistency – finding the same people there; people they recognize; people who recognize them.

The impact on recruitment here is clear. It is vital to seek out and favour the kinds of people who can do that best. And, for those many companies in the process of restructuring, breaking down their hierarchies and flattening out, this presents a hard task. The temptation in such cases is to take the middle management and redeploy them at the front end, thus, as in the case of IBM in the early 1990s, increasing the number of people available to deal with Customers in one context or another. Yet, the fact is that many people who have been obsessed, sometimes for years, with the internal workings of the company may have become corporate introverts. That is to say, the corporation, to whose welfare they have been dedicated for so long, assumes greater importance to them than the well-being or goodwill of the Customer.

Consider how this affects them. For example, if you look at the difference in approach towards a late payer between someone in the accounts department and someone on the sales team, you'll appreciate my comment. One sees the Customer as a lawbreaker dedicated to withholding money that rightly belongs with their employer, and causing cash-flow problems; the other is trying to tread on eggshells, knowing he has to get the money in, but not wanting to risk the next order by raising awkward subjects or by threatening. Neither one of these is wrong, and yet they both are. They have to get the money in. So, in both cases, it is right objectives, wrong mentality.

In relationship building, the mentality of the individuals towards the Customer is critical. To some extent this can be dealt with by training, but one is also inevitably looking for the actual capacity and propensity within that individual to relate to other human beings. And particularly to Customers, the most important human beings there are! Thus we learn that the delivery of quality to Customers starts with quality people. Quality, not just in the sense of how they perform against conventional targets, but how well they perform in their human interactions; how good they are at building and sustaining relationships that work.

Effectively, all of this tells you that many of the staff you would ideally like to redeploy while restructuring may not have the necessary people skills, even though they have experience of your business in abundance. People skills can be enhanced by training, but they cannot easily and successfully be implanted or bestowed on someone who just doesn't have them in the first place. If a place cannot be found for such staff, where they will not be damaging or inhibiting, they must be compassionately assisted in moving on to new pastures.

Increased training levels

The biggest problem for people in these new flatter structures is that the training ground (previously, to a large extent, encountered in climbing the corporate hierarchy) has disappeared just at a time when the new objectives require even greater levels of training, coaching and mentoring.

Thus it will be important to ensure that workloads and timetables leave adequate time for training and education; that the resources, facilities and budget are available; and that the motivation is there for the training to be accepted and adopted by those who participate.

There's no escape. We all have to deliver

The Customer's expectation of satisfactory service, both as a consumer and a business, is about to go through the roof. Smart businesses are already planning their superformance. They are adopting the kind of techniques I call 'Success through Excess'. Six-sigma comes to service! It is no longer adequate merely to meet Customers' expectations. Customer superformance is the name of the game. That's where you'll find the miracles on the trees waiting to be picked. If, like Tesco, you have some Harrys, encourage and empower them. Let them build the Customer relationships for you. It is well worth every penny or cent on every phone call. Tear down the barriers between you and your Customers. Don't be like the Swede who, when asked why he was attending one of my sessions in Stockholm, told me, 'I have to find a way to get my Customers to call in with their orders after 10am and before 4pm. Otherwise we'll never have time to run the business and take care of the administration!' It didn't take long for him to realize that fewer Customers equalled less administration, and no Customers equalled no administration! Let them order when they want. Cope with the administration any other time.

During the 1960s, the quantity drive brought the benefits of mass production, competitive pricing and wider availability. Consumers, used to post-war austerity throughout the world, revelled in being able to obtain a range of goods such as they had never experienced before. Credit became more readily available and the Age of Plenty was well under way. In relative terms, the Age of Plenty has now become the Age of Sufficiency. Household equipment in most Western European countries extends to TV, refrigerator, telephone, washing machine, video, microwave and dishwasher, with many other things considered basic necessities. And that's before you step outside the home. As consumers become more experienced, so, quite justifiably, they become more sophisticated, more aware and concerned about their rights, and much, much harder to please. Why? Because they've now observed several decades of the contortions sales and marketing people will go to in the process of obtaining their business, and they know that, because they hold the purse, they call the tune. There is nothing wrong with this. It is right and proper that they should feel this way.

Moreover, watching consumerist and pressure groups, most particularly in Europe, I am now convinced of the surfacing of suspicion, anger and resentment aimed at the processes of sales, advertising and marketing, and at the people who practise them. This is all caused by the abandoning of quality, the greed of quantity-driven marketing, and years of being subjected to exploitation selling processes.

Now I know that, in the USA particularly, selling has a very different image from that in Europe. In Australasia and South Africa, it lies somewhere between the two. But where in the world do people implicitly trust, respect and have total faith in sales and marketing people? Nowhere I've been. I mean, we may all be jolly nice people, easy to get on with, fun to talk with…but who trusts us? Whose interest do our Customers think we put first – ours or theirs? It is strange really, because my mother trusted her grocer. When and why did Customers stop trusting the people who sold to them? And the pivotal issue that determines the need for Customer-driven strategies is how we can regain that respect and trust. The solutions to these questions are easy to identify, but more difficult to implement. Regaining the respect and trust of the Customer is a magnificent and extremely profitable Customer-driven miracle.

Why have the new demands of the Customer become a global issue?

The first reason is the way the media network their programmes around the globe these days. Suppose you're watching CNN in a hotel in Copenhagen (or on cable in your sitting room at home); you're watching a news clip of some new shopping innovation in Australia; you now want it, and you know you can have it. Your assessment of your local shops is measured against the local shops from Helsinki to Vancouver to Auckland.

Second, as technology and design find similar answers to the same old questions, the parity products issue forces corporations to look at other ways of securing business. Customer service, Customer care and the added-value route will turn up the heat.

Third, Customers are becoming increasingly sophisticated and informed. They will, naturally, become more discerning and hold greater expectations. The only real dilemmas are not whether you should do it, whether it will do you good, or whether your Customers will like it. The dilemmas are how you will fund these new service and care levels, and what will happen to you if you don't.

I am not going to delve deeply into the practical aspects of Customer service or Customer care programmes, for this is not a book about these subjects. However, it is a book about the need for them. And, in order to practise the art of Customer-driven business, one must become a master of Customer service and Customer care. The building of a Customer relationship is rather like the building of a strong brick wall. Its deep and secure foundations lie in its philosophy, culture and commitment to Customers. The bricks are the individual sales or units of sales. The cement is the loyalty that is created in that Customer. It holds the sales process together, bonding between the individual sales, creating strength and resilience. The water, sand and mortar from which that cement is made are Customer satisfaction, Customer service and Customer care. Becoming Customer-driven is, in effect, a safe and secure place for your company to weather the storms of the business world. Now you know how the walls to that safe place must be built. Simple, really. It's all about Customers.

In thinking about the new objectives, directions and thinking of the marketer, we have considered the following:

- Customer-driven marketing requires the building of stable and rewarding Customer relationships. Customer service must have strategic integrity and be built into the system. It must be practised by all, from the top down, with no exceptions, no excuses.
- Companies that build relationships not sales stand out from the crowd. They attract and receive vastly increased levels of loyalty, affection, respect and trust.
- Customer service and quality standards went into rapid and severe decline during the 1960s and 1970s.
- An example was given in which the harnessing of technology and marketing skills was able to return the quality and individual treatment to relationships to a great extent whilst maintaining the scale and quantities required today.
- By the end of the 1980s, we had moved from the Age of Plenty to the Age of Sufficiency. Customers had taken control of their spending. They have freedom, they have choice, and they have legs. They will use all three increasingly.
- Consumers the world over view marketing and the marketing process with suspicion and distrust. This must change, but it must be a real change. It's no good polishing our smile and our armour. We have to learn to listen, to respect and to practise our handshake.
- The three major influences that will spread the word as far as what the Customer can get are:

- the media: the global village is full of gossips;
- parity products: Customer service gives an attractive edge and it's difficult to withdraw it;
- the Customer is more sophisticated and informed and, as a result, more discerning and demanding.
- From a sound relationship, sales and loyalty are cultivated together. Customer-driven businesses use Customer satisfaction, Customer service and Customer care for the bonding process.
- Whereas the old-fashioned sales techniques are on the decline, Customer-driven techniques are on the increase. Much of this softer, more professional style has to do with the longer-term objectives that result.

4

The facts and fallacies of Customer loyalty

I suspect that many business experts of our time are taking simple long-held knowledge and beliefs and making them more complex than they actually are. Many, it is certain, manage to find ways of explaining and describing fundamental truths in the most complex ways. In relation to Customer satisfaction and Customer loyalty there seems to be much of this going on. I remain undecided as to whether it really does become more complex as we move further into the soft issues, and as the genuine intricacies of the human psychological aspects come into closer focus, or whether my peers and I are guilty of complicating very simple issues. Maybe a deal of both is true – I will leave you to decide for yourself as you digest this chapter.

The waitress was a singer

I was on the road home. It was late and I was hungry. I sat in the rather shabby branch of a chain of UK roadside restaurants. I chewed my way through a very tasteless and rather chewy piece of steak. It was marginally better than staying hungry. About half-way through, the young waitress who had taken my order, and served me, reappeared. She sang to me, 'Is everything allllriiight?'

I don't know who teaches these people, who are mostly young, to sing to their Customers. Switchboard operators and receptionists do it a lot too. It's as if they somehow equate the singing tone and extended vowels with a caring attitude. I looked at her, smiled and replied, 'Yes, it's fine, thank you.' She had just sampled Customer satisfaction. The truth was that the steak was well below acceptable and I was actually toying with the idea of re-soling a pair of favourite old shoes with the remains of it. My real reply should have been, 'No. It's awful and I'm not coming here again.' Customer loyalty index? Zero.

Well, why didn't I tell her? Because, because. Because I was tired. Because she was at the end of her shift. They were waiting to close. I couldn't be bothered. It wasn't her fault. And so on. And so on. You know how it is! But I still won't go back there.

This is an important point and, for me, renders tenuous Customer satisfaction (what I say – 'Yes, it's fine, thank you'), and leaves it deeply subordinate to Customer loyalty (what I do – 'I'm not coming here again'). There are plenty of people who will tell you that satisfaction levels are linked to loyalty levels. I find that rather like saying that a swimming pool *looks* warm enough. There is nothing better than actually sticking a toe in and feeling it to find out. Of course they are linked. There would be little loyalty without Customer satisfaction. However, some leading consultancies have given advice to their Clients that would seem to propose that managing Customer satisfaction is enough. It is not. Later in this chapter we will see that it is just one of the components. You have to get Customers well towards the very top end of satisfaction levels before there is any kind of robustness, and loyalty is created.

The inescapable truth of Customer loyalty and the five strands that create it

Loyalty is, inescapably, the truth of your success as a business. There is no more telling benchmark by which you can be measured and judged. It is the sum total of the effect of your business or organization on its Customers, and their response to it. This means that 'the Customer' is, and must always be, the reason for your existence. There is no other reason. In business there is no other purpose. This is the inexorable rationale for the Customer-driven business. It explains, for all those business leaders who can't seem to make up their minds, why it is quite wrong to stand up in front of staff and tell them that they are the most important asset of the business. They clearly are not. It's the Customer who has to be first and foremost because, without Customers, who needs staff? Business leaders with enough money can certainly have as many staff as they like with no Customers at all. Employees definitely follow next in priority, for, without loyal and passionate staff, any attempt at Customer loyalty or becoming Customer-driven is doomed to fail.

Satisfaction may be a vital component part of Customer loyalty, yet satisfied Customers leave your business and defect as well as dissatisfied Customers. More confusing still, loyal Customers leave you too. In fact, my wife and I have just parted company with a host of traders, shops and services to whom we were totally loyal, and about whom we would still give excellent word-of-mouth referrals. We just moved house and changed area.

The five strands to Customer satisfaction and loyalty are, however, common. They are:

- price;
- product;
- delivery;
- service; and
- recognition.

Each strand needs careful thought. I have a PowerPoint slide that lists them. In order to make a point, I listed them with the first two (price and product) in white, and the last two (service and recognition) in red. Delivery is in half-white and half-red. 'Why?', I ask my audiences, 'do you think delivery is half-white and half-red?'

The answer is not that I'm no good at using PowerPoint, as someone proposed recently. No, Sir!

So what is the answer? It's that the issues wrapped round the first two and a half strands – price, product and some delivery issues – are based in logic. The other two and a half – the remainder of delivery, service and recognition – are based in emotion. For the last 30 years, marketing has obsessed itself with the first two and a half. Now, in order to concentrate on Customer relationships, you have to get your business to become excellent at delivering the emotionally based issues.

You are what you eat!

You may have heard that expression used about food. Eat fat, get fat, they say. Well, the same applies to your business. So, if you sell on price, you attract people who buy on price. If they buy on price, next time they'll buy the cheapest, which might be elsewhere. If you want to be the bargain basement of your particular market, go for it! If not, beware! Customers who come for price, go for price. They have little long-term loyalty potential.

Customer loyalty and Customer satisfaction share the same five strands, which entwine like the strands of a rope. They are as follows:

Price

There's no getting away from price. It is always there, in what I call 'the value balance'. However, we very often over-rate the importance of price – or, worse still, we actually exacerbate it. If you are generally a discount or bargain basement operation, that's fine. If not, you are simply eroding your own margins by promoting on price. This does not stop you promoting on value. But get price in perspective. One of the long-term reasons for adopting a Customer loyalty strategy is that it shrinks price in the Customer's priority and replaces it with value.

Product

There is no substitute for delivering a quality product. If the product fails, breaks down, doesn't last as long as it should, or is in any way imperfect, Customers will not come back for more. Nor will they feel inclined to buy other things from you. One of the stark realizations a Customer-driven business has to make from the very beginning is that there are no hiding places. Customer loyalty is built by *exceeding* Customer expectations at every opportunity.

Delivery

If you are an 'old-school' marketer or salesperson, familiar with the old textbooks, this is what used to be called 'distribution'. If you have some of the old textbooks, throw them away or hide them in the loft. Business has changed so much over the last few years that the old ideas no longer work.

Delivery includes distribution but it encompasses far more. Think of it as the delivery of the whole corporate promise to the Customer. By this I mean every facet of the way the Customer feels, touches and experiences your business. This includes the way the call centre or switchboard deals with Customers, the wording on your packaging, owners' manuals or handbooks, the impact of your invoices and stationery, the way you announce price increases, your attitude to 'green' issues and genetic modification of food, if appropriate. Everything makes an impression on a Customer, so make sure it's a great impression.

The significant difference between distribution and delivery is the realization that, when you are in business to achieve a series of separate transactions, those transactions take place at the far point of your distribution channel. This is a product-driven process. It distributes your corporate product or service. When you are in business to achieve a managed Customer relationship, then what we have is a means of delivering the corporate promise. Transaction marketing effectively switches on to standby between transactions; relationship marketing is permanently fully switched on 24 hours a day, seven days a week, ready and alert to every Customer interaction wherever it touches the organization.

Service

In a Customer-driven business, service is paramount – but by now you should be getting the impression that everything is paramount, which is why I maintain that a Customer loyalty strategy must obsess the whole business. If you are a small business, this is good news. Both size and traditional structures inhibit larger businesses in delivering service. Smaller companies don't have nearly so many protocols and are much less set in their ways. If a Customer wants something different or special, the smaller company can just do it.

Does this mean that a big business cannot become a Customer-driven business? Certainly not! But it does mean it has more, and more serious, issues to address: management culture, organizational structure and human resources, to name but a few. In short, they have to retain the advantages of size and lose the disadvantages. Lumbering giants have to become as agile and fleet of foot as their smaller competitors.

Recognition

Whether you're thinking about Customer loyalty and becoming a Customer-driven organization for business-to-business or business-to-consumer, the rudiments of developing and managing Customer loyalty are exactly the same. We all love to be recognized not just for who we are, but for other things about us.

Some of the most significant contributions I have seen to the loyalty-building process have come from streaming consistent groups of employees to consistent groups of Customers. The result is that the two groups become familiar and their relationships have a far greater chance of success. They know each other!

To boost Customer loyalty, we therefore need to work on continuous improvement of the corporate promise, and that means all five strands. Our previous experiences were logic based – product, price and some delivery issues (essentially those to do with distribution). We need to supplement them with new, 'soft issue' experiences, which are emotionally based; these include service, recognition and those corporate delivery issues that surround the product at distribution, and stay connected with the Customer throughout their relationship with us. Now we have to examine how we leave Customers feeling.

For those who worry that this is new and different, it is not. It has been done before – but not in the volume and at the speed required today. For my parents, for example, the kind of things we are discussing in this book were not only the ideals to which they worked, they were what they expected – and got. Even if it was low-tech or no-tech!

To move from building satisfaction to creating loyalty, you must work in the emotional issues of the relationship. This will gain the most leverage and make the most difference. Miracle after miracle is to be found here. It is this recognition that exposes the fallacy in the vast majority of so-called 'loyalty programmes'.

Bribery and integrity are like oil and water. They don't mix!

Most loyalty programmes rely, to a major degree, on bribery. This is like the villain in a children's pantomime handing out sweets to the goodie in the show. None of the kids in the audience are fooled. They don't trust the villain's smile or voice.

I ask some of my audiences to examine the difference between a personal relationship and a commercial relationship. I 'marry' someone from the audience. (I say 'someone'. I've never picked on a man!) Anyway, I use entertaining role-play to look at the phases of the relationship and to highlight the similarities.

Lately, I have taken to 'surveying' the same audiences as follows: first, I ask those who have a loyalty card to raise their hand. Then I ask those who do not have two or more loyalty cards for the same type of business – supermarket, hotel group, airline, whatever – to lower their hand. Last, I ask those whose hand remains raised which of them uses all the businesses, and frequently gathers loyalty bonuses from all the programmes? Many hands are still up. So, which one are they being loyal to?

My next question is, 'If you found your partner had two other people to whom he or she was also being "loyal" on a regular basis, would you consider that he or she was also being "faithful"? If you do, keep your hands up.' Not one hand has stayed up yet.

Most 'loyalty programmes' are heavily disguised sales promotions, which use the mail and the shop and whatever to merchandise special offers and discounts. It's basically good old-fashioned bribery! It has nothing at all to do with gathering the emotional commitment of the Customer so that they bestow their allegiance to you. It has nothing or little to do with winning over the heart and mind of Customers.

The truth is that, at best, all these schemes create is a bond. It's just a link, not a lock. Some may manage to create quite a strong bond. Yet the major benefit of such schemes is that they tend to increase exposure to, and sampling of, the corporate promise. As I use my airline miles or store card bonus points, I often use them for more of what I have been getting already. I'll fly somewhere on holiday, or buy something that means the operator of the loyalty scheme gets another chance to prove its worth.

So, what wins hearts and minds?

Certainly, there is a place for discounts and special deals if they fit with your mission and your brand(s). However, the bulk of the loyalty-building solutions will be found in the soft issues to do with service and recognition. It may occasionally be considered right or prudent to issue money-off vouchers or make discount offers, but the style and tone of voice with which they are distributed on those occasions is important.

It is in delivering those aspects of the corporate promise to do with service and recognition that hearts and minds will be won over – in recognizing and treating Customers as the individuals they are, in knowing their preferences and choices, and in understanding what turns them on or off. This builds loyalty – and it also creates a 'quality lock', which locks them to you and locks your competitor out. Further, knowing Customers' preferences – indeed, accumulating and actively using information in recognition of Customers – means that Customers have taken you through a learning cycle about themselves. They have, effectively, trained you to look after them. That should make you easier and more convenient to deal with, and others less so. It is a sort of golden ring-fence. It keeps the Customer with you and the others out. It is part of the quality lock that locks them to you and locks your competitors out. A miracle in itself.

Switching to a loyalty mind-set means turning much more attention on your Customers. They won't become more loyal unless you devote more time and effort to them. But the result is not just a good warm feeling, it is increased sales at far lower costs. That's why you have to get into the loyalty business.

I remember being asked to carry out a marketing audit for a financial service business in the UK. They felt they had incredibly 'loyal' Customers. They had over 150,000 policyholders, of whom only 7,000 had bought more than one product. Now they may have had a good image with Customers; they may have had great Customer satisfaction; but loyalty? They were kidding themselves.

To get into the loyalty business, you have to do loyalty work. Loyalty work is real. It happens in Customers' lives. It's attentive to Customers and it builds far more for you than any disguised bribery via a simple loyalty club, programme, or scheme. Why? Because Customers feel it, experience it, and value it. It's a much more tangible demonstration of the way you value them and their custom than a few mailings and a sporadic dissemination of discount vouchers from manufacturers you have been able to do deals with. Customers have been there and done that. It's called the past. Customers realize that what is happening now is about them; it is driven by and for their needs, aspirations and desires – and it is happening in tune with their lives.

Loyalty is so much more robust than satisfaction. It permits dialogue. It tolerates flaws as long as they are sensitively handled, tangible action is taken to avoid them happening again, and the apologies are sincere.

Following spinal surgery, I acquired a new workstation and chair, which enabled me to continue to work the long hours that I do at my PC. The screen and keyboard were in a raised position, encouraging me to sit correctly for my spine. It was a self-build or 'flat-pack', which I quickly constructed with the simplest of instructions – the only kind that are any good for me! To the right of the keyboard support was a mouse shelf, which, try as I might, I could not get to stay in position. One day, since the manufacturer was local, I decided to take the relevant faulty parts to them. I was greeted with profuse apologies, offered coffee and asked to wait a few minutes. Shortly, the factory manager arrived carrying the unit, which now had its mouse tray correctly attached. He told me, 'I want you to know how grateful we are to you for taking the time to visit us and bring us this defective product. I can assure you defects are rare but you have enabled us to uncover a batch of keyboard supports that have brackets three milli-metres out of alignment. Thanks to you, we can contact the relevant dealers and recall the units and rescue our reputation for perfection. I have a meeting in ten minutes time with my production team to see how we can stop such an error happening again.' More pleasantries followed and I went on my way a happy Customer. I'd buy from them again – or recommend them to anyone.

The Customer-driven business model: the myriad of miracles that await you

You should think about the Customer-driven business model as a loy-alty machine. Get your business running this way, get your act right, and Customer loyalty is the natural end result. When you look at the machine, you'll find it has three principal areas. The top area is about the acquisition of new business. The left-hand side is about looking after Customers and fulfilling all their needs. The central core – I think of it as the engine of the Customer loyalty machine – is Cus-tomer superformance: the ability of your business to create the WOW factor at every interaction with Customers. Finally, to the right are issues concerning complaint handling and resolution.

I have numbered the panels in the model and the numbers relate to the paragraphs that follow. Effectively, now you have a step-by-step guide to building and managing real Customer loyalty. It is a step-by-step guide to a Customer-driven business.

The 17 key issues for Customer loyalty

This is a model for a business devoted to and obsessed with Customer loyalty. You can see the additional benefits of this devotion and obsession around the sides of the model: lower costs, improved brand performance and increased business efficiency. This is a veritable treasure chest of untapped potential for your business. Look at the issues that rain (sideways rain!) on improved brand performance. On the other side, more rain! This time showering improvements to costs and, meanwhile, every issue leads to eventual increased business efficiencies.

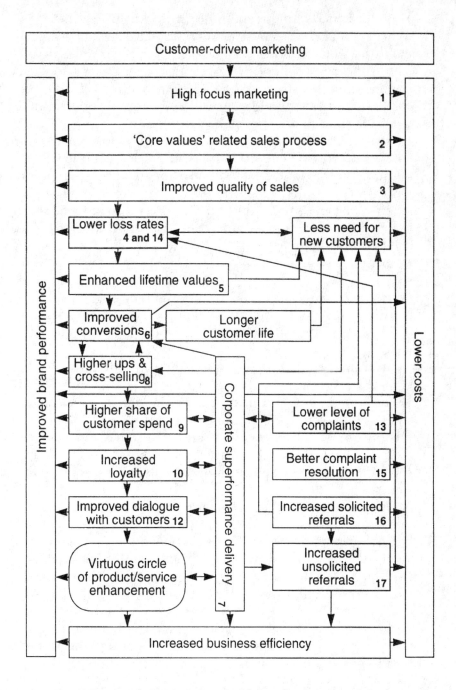

Figure 4.1 JFR's Customer-driven business model

1. High-focus marketing is the process of focusing on those Customers in your prospective market which have the highest potential loyalty for you. These can be modelled out from analysis of your Customer database. The strategic concept here is to secure dominant market share of those Customers who 'lock' with your core corporate and brand values – those things that differentiate you from your competition. The essential you.

2. In turn, naturally, you must then embed those core values into your sales process. This optimizes the 'fit' between the way you attract Customers and what they want – or are buying – from you.

3. Once you get that fit, there is a dramatic improvement in the quality of business that you gain. Effectively, you are now taking the cream from the marketplace and leaving the rest for your competitors to fight over.

4. In turn, this has two effects that will be of enormous benefit for your business: first, higher loyalty means lower Customer attrition; second, this will be a major factor in reducing sales costs. If you are losing less business you will not need such high levels of prospecting – you will cut back radically on the very high costs it incurs.

5. Next, from the model, you can see the natural follow-on is that Customer lifetime values are enhanced. If you haven't already started calculating and using lifetime values, I do encourage you to do so. The use of lifetime values seems to be almost like turning on a light to so many of those who remain unconvinced by the ethical, moral, cultural or philosophical rationales for rebuilding their business around the Customer. More on lifetime values follows.

Once you have defined and calculated your measures of lifetime values, you can start the process of managing them and beginning to appreciate the full benefits of what can be achieved. You will get two significant uplifts from managing Customer lifetime values upwards. First, you will find that the conversion-to-sale ratios are improved by about double. You can imagine the effect this has on sales costs. They tumble! Second, you will find that simply being aware of, and managing, the process of Customer lifetime values brings the in-built benefit of extending them.

Now that the light is turned on and you can really see what's what, the argument for delivering Customer superformance – actually exceeding Customer expectations with every transaction and interaction – begins to make supreme sense. It is only when you look a the financial dynamics of lifetime values that a lot of the things you must do for loyalty building become affordable. Trying to run a business devoted to Customer loyalty but costing it against single transactions doesn't work. If you make the shift, the debate about whether Customers deserve, or are worth it, just falls away.

6. Now to the earnest business of prolonging Customer 'life' by keeping them deliriously, constantly and actively satisfied with your business, the service and values you deliver, and the products that you make or distribute. This should become a permanent quest, which preoccupies and obsesses all staff. The obsession applies whether they are Customer-facing or not. Customer superformance is a benign and wonderful concept. It must take place at every opportunity and in every area. It will bring nothing but prosperity, growth and profit to your business.

7. You are about to kick-start your business into the next phase of its development in becoming Customer-driven. Those improved conversion ratios pay off with much higher incidences of cross- and up-selling to your existing Customers – these are the easiest, least expensive sales your business can achieve. Later, I will explain just how dramatically this step can work for you. It is quite common for the movement of activity and resource away from 'cold' conquest or prospecting to focus on existing Customers to improve return on investment by 5 to 15 times – an average of a tenfold improvement.

8. With the simultaneous effect of Customer superformance and improved conversion rates yielding more cross- and up-selling, we find the all-important share of Customer spend increases rapidly. This is a great loyalty builder and a great way of measuring the success of your loyalty work.

9. Now you will start to see the loyalty factor climbing to levels you would only ever have dreamed of before – if you had been ready or able to measure it.

10. As the natural result, you have a vastly improved dialogue with Customers and this will begin returning benefits to you. They value you because you have amply demonstrated that you care about and value them. The word 'natural' here is interesting because, if you look at the model, you will see how naturally these steps fit together. Given that you perform and listen and deliver, everything fits holistically and harmoniously into a natural

order. It is this natural quality of the process that gives it such elegance, and which makes it as right for you as it is for your Customers.

11. With the dialogue between you and your Customers enabling discussion, debate and free exchanges about their needs and feelings, and encouraging honest, frank feedback regarding your efforts for them, you now arrive at a virtuous circle of product and service enhancement. With openness abounding, and debate and discussion taking place, you can 'sit' with your Customers and discuss the future. You can discuss what you are getting right and wrong, what they want and don't want, and what their views and feelings are. This will yield a wealth of new product and process development ideas and activities. In turn, you can ask Customers for opinion and counsel. They feel involved, heard and recognized. And you can discuss all your new ideas with them.

12. Turning to the model again, observe what is happening to the right of the Customer superformance panel. Once you turn the spotlight on to amazing your Customers at every opportunity, and exceeding their perception of service and value, you will find complaints plummet to all-time lows. This is good news and bad news! On the one hand, it is obviously good news – Customers are happy with you and what you are doing for them. On the other hand, it is bad news, because complaints are valuable opportunities to build Customer loyalty.

   As you manage complaint figures down, notice how this contributes to a further reduction in your Customer-loss rate (on the left-hand side towards the top of the chart).

13. Handling complaints efficiently and effectively, of course, gives you valuable experience in how to react to unhappy Customers. The more you learn, and the faster you act, the better you should become at complaint resolution.

14. All of this, supported by the radically improving standards in Customer superformance, brings you another naturally flowing benefit. Moving back to the lower left panels of the chart, we see how, once we have started genuinely to work the loyalty spell, we can actually – gently and sensitively – ask the Customer to help us. We can ask them to provide us with referrals.

15. Then, finally, we gain the full benefit of what I described earlier as the cheapest, most effective advertising you can buy – word of mouth. These are the unsolicited testimonials with which

Customers reward those with whom they are wholly content, those who get it right, leaving them actively satisfied. They are so supremely happy, they want to tell the world about you.

Notice this!

Before we finish this piece on JFR's Customer-driven business model, let me ask you to notice one or two more things. These are positively magic qualities for your business and perhaps the secret of the success of the whole concept of Customer loyalty and a Customer-driven business. At the beginning of this section I listed the additional outcomes as follows:

● improved brand performance;
● lower costs; and
● increased business efficiency.

I'd like you to look at the number of arrows that point to increased brand efficiency and, equally, at the number that point to lower costs. And for that matter, while you're counting arrows, it wouldn't do any harm to note that there are quite a few pointing to the panel 'less need for new Customers'! Also note that everything in the chart moves towards increased business efficiency. That's why I describe this process as benign, virtuous and holistic. It is as near as you will get to organic. It enhances the life of all it touches. That is why it works. It simply returns the dynamics of the business to 're-set'.

Introducing lifetime values

To increase Customer loyalty it is important to shift from thinking about Customers as units of transaction – single sales – and to start treating them as individuals with whom you want to have a Customer relationship for life. 'Life' in this context may not mean for the whole of the Customer's life – but, in some cases, it might.

One of the world's largest motor manufacturers worked out that the true value of a new Customer was not just the purchase of their next car, but was actually over £400,000. They realized that if you add in all the potential repeat purchases, all the servicing, all the finance, all the extras – if they got their act right all the way through – that was the potential value to the brand. Seeing an individual Customer as a potential Customer lifetime value of £400,000, rather than just as a £15,000 transaction, can lead to some valuable shifts in thinking.

Thinking about the value of that Customer to your business for the long term enables you to reconsider your attitudes, tactics, marketing, thinking, service – everything!

How do you measure loyalty?

Loyalty at its heart – what people do as opposed to what people say – can be measured by their ultimate doing: their buying behaviour. However, to limit yourself to this is like planning a journey by the distance, taking no account of what the road is like. To get the full picture, we need to access Customers' feelings as well as their actions. The problem here is that Customers, particularly disgruntled Customers, don't talk to you, and don't share their feelings.

British Airways carried out its own research into this, discovering that only eight per cent of Customers talked to its Customer Relations people about the quality of service, whether their experience was good or bad. A further 24 per cent did share their feelings with someone but the information never reached Customer relations; and the majority, 68 per cent, didn't talk to 'anybody'. I think they mean anybody at the airline, for my experience suggests that the happy Customers do talk to two or three people, and the unhappy ones to four to six times as many. British Airways decided, as a result, to facilitate the process and encourage Customers to talk to them in greater numbers. They set up Customer listening posts, which included internationally toll-free surveys, Customer forums held and attended by BA executives, and the placing of Customer relations personnel on flights together with Customers. Their data, after all, had shown that, for every £1 invested in Customer retention, they received £2 back.

Taking this whole matter very seriously, British Airways then installed an image-based computer system to enable global access to Customer case histories and to eliminate paperwork. It re-engineered its Customer service process down from 13 steps to 3; empowered its Customer relations teams to use whatever resources were required to retain the Customer; and invested in interpersonal skills training to improve the handling of Customers.

In a similar way, I have encouraged a number of my Clients to develop programmes that reward staff for uncovering Customer complaints or grievances. It is important, though, that staff who uncover complaints also have the power to do more than just hear and sympathize with the Customer.

Customer complaint handling is now a 3-step process at British Airways. Step 1 is to apologize and get an individual to own the problem; Step 2 is to resolve the complaint quickly – the target is the same day, and 3 days is the longest acceptable; Step 3 is to convince the Customer that the problem is being fixed to stop it happening again. BA encourages staff to do as many as possible of the steps by phone.

The following three figures are the results of a Customer survey carried out by one of my Clients. They demonstrate that there is a very tangible link between loyalty and the intent to repurchase. I see this intent as a valuable measure of loyalty.

Satisfaction level	% definitely/probably buy again
Very satisfied	95
Satisfied	66
Less than satisfied	14

Figure 4.2 Customer superformance guarantees repeat sales

Satisfaction level following problem resolution	% definitely/probably buy again
Satisfied	76 (over 5 times 'dissatisfied')
Mollified	34
Dissatisfied	14

Figure 4.3 Resolving Customers' problems is vital for future business

Satisfaction level following problem resolution	% definitely/probably buy again
Satisfied (30%)	76
Mollified (50%)	34
Dissatisfied (20%)	14
Unresolved (37%)	21

Figure 4.4 Effective problem recovery is powerfully good for sales (as well as relationships)

From Figures 4.2, 4.3 and 4.4, we can see that this Client was in a rather unhappy state and there was plenty of work to be done. Figure 4.2 shows that it was no different from the rest of the world. Its Customers confirmed that 95 per cent of them, if they were actively satisfied, would buy again. Figure 4.3 demonstrates that a satisfied Customer is more than five times as likely to buy again. Figure 4.4 shows that (bottom left) 37 per cent of the Client's Customer problems were unresolved at the time of the survey. This is quite a frightening figure! Of the 100 per cent whose problems had been resolved, 30 per cent were satisfied, 50 per cent were mollified and 20 per cent were dissatisfied. I suspect the 14 per cent of Customers expressing dissatisfaction were probably prepared to buy again because they had earlier enjoyed a different experience, and this demonstrates that Customers have a certain degree of tolerance. Or it may just be that they don't feel that they would get any better anywhere else! You will notice that the figure of the unresolved who would buy again is higher than those whose complaint had been resolved unsatisfactorily – that is plainly because a number of them were still waiting in line to become dissatisfied!

The figures in these tables were used widely within the organization both to convince senior executives that they should invest heavily and quickly in their equivalent of a Customer superformance programme, and to demonstrate to sales and marketing people that a rapid change of culture, style and method was vital, and long overdue. The picture was probably actually worse than stated here, and as revealed by the survey. My experience suggests that these figures usually overstate the case of repurchase. In the USA, research confirms this. Somewhere between 60 to 80 per cent of automobile purchasers, interviewed 90 days after a purchase, said they would buy the same brand again yet, three to four years later, only 35 to 40 per cent actually do. The moral is clear – stay in touch and superform at every opportunity. If the opportunities don't arise, create them.

The checklist of loyalty measures

Here's a checklist of the most popular measures. However, if your business finds other ways, add or substitute them:

- customer satisfaction – what they say;
- recency – when they last purchased;
- frequency – how often they purchase;
- monetary value – how much they spend;
- Customer longevity – how long they have been with you;
- formal and informal (word of mouth) referral activity;
- share of spend – how much to you and how much to competitors; and
- willingness to repurchase.

Share of spend

If you consciously work to build your share of the available and appropriate 'wallet' for that family, household or business, suddenly the whole picture is transformed. If most businesses had anything like 75 per cent of the available spend of its Customers, annual targets would be met in the first month! Most businesses neglect Customers and, as a result, Customers place business elsewhere. When looking at how much they spend, remember to consider current and recent transactions, and to keep a cumulative figure too.

Share of spend shares a characteristic with Customer satisfaction and with Customer loyalty. All three are comparatively fragile until you are reaching levels of approximately 70-80 per cent. Up to that level, Customers are still very vulnerable to competitive offers and propositions; at lower than 50 per cent, there is no significant value. With share of available spend, I normally find that at 75 per cent of the Customers' available spend, you can feel reasonably safe in that you know you have secured their trust, their loyalty and their affection. 'Available spend', with a business, would probably be a budget for that product or service. With a consumer, it is either their appropriate, affordable or desired amount. Often this is a notional assessment but you can easily ask the Customer for pointers.

Finally, how far will they go to help you?

Another valuable piece of information is whether Customers will do anything positive or negative to assist you – whether they ever pass on positive or negative word of mouth, or are prepared to give solicited referrals or testimonials. With these questions, you are deep into the heart of soft-issue country. Often, you will find that Customers are in fact more open and more honest about whether they would recommend you to someone else than they are about whether they would buy from you again.

Nine steps to managing Customer loyalty

Let's look together at the nine steps you should take to build and manage loyalty for your business.

1. Define, then manage loyalty
    Every business has its own ideas of what is meant by loyalty and, probably, different shades of it. Create your own definition, but be very sure that your definition includes measurable performance indicators. Use the ideas for measurement in the checklist earlier and decide which, if not all, of those are appropriate for your business, and/or add your own.
        Remember, if you can't measure loyalty, then you can't manage it. You're driving blind! Set your sights high. Your task is to exceed Customers' expectations at every interaction because this will lead to active satisfaction, which is far more powerful and builds loyalty.
2. Understand the economics of loyalty
    Here's what happens. Price sensitivity goes down. Referrals go up. Sales costs go down. But you need to know by how much. Start with a clear audit of what's happening now, otherwise you won't know just how you are doing. If it's possible, audit the business Customer by Customer. If not, use the smallest possible homogeneous groups. To provide an effective audit you should take soundings on the same performance indicators that you built in to your definition in Step 1.

3. Segment and identify potential high-loyalty Customers
    Are you choosing the right Customers? This concept surprises
    people and I still don't know why. You have to be choosy about
    who you allow to be a Customer of yours. Most businesses go at
    markets as if they were vacuum cleaners. They'll suck up any-
    thing. The fact is that most businesses have Customers who range
    in value – some are extremely profitable, some are loss making
    and on some you may be lucky to break even. If you can't manage
    those in the last two groups successfully into profit, politely and
    sensitively move them on.

4. Re-focus marketing investment and acquisition activity
    accordingly
    Now you have cleaned out your Customer base, examine the
    exquisite remainder closely. This is your most valuable group of
    Customers – the ones who are your most profitable. What do you
    see? Look for facts about them that they have in common –
    things such as age, gender, location, income, wealth and job
    type. Or, if it's a business, size, sector, and so on. Make up a pro-
    file of these Customers and you now have a profile of the kind of
    Customers who have the highest loyalty potential for you. Aren't
    these the Customers you most want? Now re-focus all your efforts
    on attracting more 'perfect' Customers to your business. What
    about the others? Let your competitors lose money on them!

    If you have a database of a reasonable size, it will pay you to
    seek help with this. If you are in consumer markets, there is a
    wealth of psychographic, demographic and other information
    that outside specialists can offer, which adds enormous accuracy
    and depth to your profiling.

5. Align personnel recruitment, motivation and rewards to Cus-
    tomer values
    Now you have to make sure your business is manned to suit these
    perfect Customers. (Before regulation, insurance businesses
    would recruit almost anyone to sell for them. Most of them would
    be the very last person you would place your savings or pension
    with.) The German chain store Netto recently explained how its
    basic market was mature adults; a survey of Customers revealed
    that those mature adults most like to be served by (surprise, sur-
    prise!) mature adults. A smart move by Netto.

    Next, look at how you motivate your people. Be particularly
    wary of commission on sales. It is perfectly good to build up the
    commission kitty from sales. But don't pay it out that way.

Dispense it against things that work for Customers – Customer satisfaction, loyalty levels, decreases in Customer-loss rates, increasing share of spend, increasing product or service sales across the range, complaint-free periods, etc. Also think about who you include with the rewards. Many more people contribute to building Customer loyalty than just the sales or marketing people. Chapter 9 is devoted to this topic.

6. Develop management thinking, processes and systems that actively improve retention rates
    Make sure that the whole business – and yes, I do mean whole business – is geared to Customer retention and development. That means accounts, personnel, everywhere. Make sure, also, that all managers realize that the most important activity happens at the front line, but that everyone's contribution is vital.

7. Probe and understand defectors' behaviour and reasoning
    Above all, go and talk to defectors! This is what I call those who decide they don't want to be your Customer any more. There are acceptable reasons for defection – moving out of the area is one. And there are unacceptable reasons – a failure of some kind, even if it is only in the Customers' perception. Failures must be removed or eradicated. And apologized for. Your long-term goal is a zero rate of the unacceptable kind of defection. Ideally, no Customer loss should occur without:
    - you knowing about it;
    - the Customer being able and encouraged to tell you why they have made that choice; and
    - learning from the experience so that any problem can be fixed.

    Lastly, the Customer should be appropriately thanked for both their help and their custom.

8. Set loyalty targets and analyse your results
    Go back to those performance indicators that were developed as part of your definition of loyalty in Step 1. Set achievable but stretching targets for these, based on the audit carried out in Step 2. Use these to analyse how well you are doing and what the trends are. The nearer you can get to doing this *per Customer*, the better. The review process should be regular and continuous. If you are not achieving targets, find out why not. What action needs to be taken? Will training or new processes improve things?

    Your review of targets should include four steps, which are a continuum: set targets; plan; act; and review.

9. Aim for continuous year-on-year improvements
    There is no going back on this one. It's what plumbers and hydraulic engineers call a non-return valve! Things can only be allowed to go one way. And every year it should get better than the last. It's not just about driving performance up – costs are supposed to be going down, service getting better, more Customer needs being met, and more data being gathered. The business is supposed to be improving in every possible way. That is one of the major benefits of driving an organization by Customer loyalty, and brings me back to one of my opening comments. Loyalty is inescapably the truth of the success of your whole business.

And don't forget the other three dimensions!

In my past, I have had very active experience of the value of building loyalty from my suppliers. And if your business is using techniques such as supply chain management, you will doubtless already have identified this issue for yourself. Frankly, attempting to gear up your business to superform for its Customers, without entering into the necessary close alliances and partnerships with your suppliers, is futile. Within a short period of time, they will seem to be living on another planet. Talk to them, involve them, gain their commitment and support – their loyalty will build as you work at the problem together, and you share the responsibilities and benefits together. Remember the power of praise. Businesses are much better at sharing negative experiences than consumers; however, businesses are much, much worse at handing out praise than they are at complaining!

In his book *The Loyalty Effect* (Harvard Business School Press, 1996), Frederick Reichheld reports that the average holding time for shares by investors has tumbled from seven years in 1960 to two years in 1996. This figure underlines how little companies do to create loyalty in their investors, which has never been more vital than it is today. Organizations needing to cope with change and market turmoil need to clutch at consistency and reliability more than ever. Without the support and loyalty of your investors, thinking long-term, or merely longer-term, is a non-starter.

Reichheld maintains that you can fish for investors who share the same qualities and ethics as your business. You should match the core Customer needs to the core values of your business to get the higher-quality, more loyal Customer. Fishing for perfect investors this way sounds a fine ideal to me – if you are a private company and can pick and choose to whom you sell your shares. If not, it's going to be considerably harder. However, there is absolutely nothing to stop you investing in communications programmes and loyalty-building activity with your shareholders – why shouldn't they, for example, be proud to own your shares as well as expect to make money from them? Equally, there is nothing to stop you using those devices that we have been discussing for Customers to analyse, measure and manage investor loyalty. Mr Reichheld seems to suggest that retaining or regaining private ownership is the answer. Again, I think this may lack a little in pragmatism, but it is right ideally. If you can't, get to work with an investor loyalty initiative – but make sure that it builds the genuine loyalty we have discussed.

And what about your people – how loyal are they?

Economically, building employee loyalty makes as much sense as building Customer loyalty. An employer with a high turnover of staff will find that recruiting new people and training them is expensive, just as recruiting new prospects and converting them to Customers is expensive. They are different sums of money, but both significant. In the same way that it is foolish to fail to build loyalty with a Customer once you have made the investment to win them, so it is also a waste of money to lose good employees once you have recruited and trained them. The development of employee loyalty is fundamental to the success of becoming Customer-driven and to delivering a sound corporate promise.

The quality of your people is vital. And the greater the reliance on technology and computerized Customer solutions, the greater, I believe, the focus must be on the people, the human element of your interactions. You must, therefore, recruit only quality people, and you must recognize that such people take their motivation, satisfaction and fulfilment from far more important things than just money. Another virtuous circle of Customer-driven businesses is that people who have the propensity to be loyal employees value and understand loyalty. Nothing will give them more pleasure and satisfaction than dealing with and cultivating that same quality in your Customers.

So, we draw to a close one of the most important and significant chapters in the desire to create miracles, to assisting your business to blossom and prosper, to building a successful future for you and for your organization. Be in no doubt: those who understand and learn and become masters at managing the four dimensions of loyalty will be among the most sought after and valued in the business world. They will have come to make their business throb to one passionate creed. It's all about Customers.

To summarize:

- Customer satisfaction is interesting to your business and will help you to understand Customer loyalty. However, ultimately, it is Customer loyalty – what people *do* as opposed to what people *say* – which is the true measure of your corporate success.
- The five strands of Customer loyalty are: in the logic area, price and product; in the emotional area, service and recognition. The fifth strand – delivery of the corporate promise – falls into both.
- Loyalty programmes relying on greed or bribery or ill-advised sales promotional techniques are unlikely to build robust, sustainable loyalty.
- The Customer-driven marketing model contains abundant miracles for your business. It demonstrates the virtuous, harmonious and natural fit of the strategy and processes, and explains how these all work together to further the brand while actually decreasing sales and marketing costs.
- The 17 steps to Customer-driven marketing clearly explain the following:
  - you should use high-focus marketing techniques to select those Customers with the highest potential for loyalty;
  - you should align your core values to the sales process;
  - this, in turn, attracts a higher-quality Customer with lower loss rates and enhanced lifetime values;
  - this leads to vastly improved sales-conversion rates with existing Customers;
  - sales costs tumble as a result;
  - being aware that lifetime values carry an inherent benefit – you start to manage and take responsibility for them, and this results in an improvement;
  - the natural consequence of the above is that you commence a programme of Customer superformance, which sets out to exceed Customer perceptions and expectations with every interaction;
  - now cross- and up-selling takes on a whole new significance to your business;
  - share of Customers is radically improved and has a marked positive effect on Customer loyalty levels;

- your dialogue with Customers becomes more valuable and useful;
- this leads to a virtuous circle of product and service enhancement;
- complaints reduce in number;
- your expertise at complaint handling grows; and
- the numbers of both solicited and unsolicited referrals increase.

- It is important to shift from thinking about Customers as units of transaction – single sales – and to start treating them as individuals with whom you want to have a Customer relationship for life. 'Life' may not mean for the whole of the Customer's life – but, in some cases, it might. Among other things, it can enable changes to attitudes, tactics, marketing, thinking and service.
- Customer loyalty is measured by Customer satisfaction; recency frequency and monetary value; Customer longevity and word-of-mouth/referral activity, and share of Customer spend.
- There are nine steps to Managing Customer loyalty:
  - define, then manage loyalty;
  - understand the economics of loyalty;
  - segment and identify potential high-loyalty Customers;
  - re-focus marketing investment and acquisition activity accordingly;
  - align personnel recruitment, motivation and rewards to Customer values;
  - develop management thinking, processes and systems that actively improve retention rates;
  - probe and understand defectors' behaviour and reasoning;
  - set loyalty targets and analyse your results;
  - aim for continuous year-on-year improvements.
- To be involved in a process of Customer superformance and loyalty building without the participation, involvement and support of your suppliers as well as Customers is a mistake and will yield failures.
- You can and should work on investor loyalty. Working on long-term Customer improvements to your business is difficult without investor support and understanding. Investors will respond similarly to Customers when you market the business to them. Their loyalty can be measured in similar ways.
- The final dimension of loyalty lies with your staff: quality of people is key. Loyal employees value and exude loyalty and will breed loyal Customers.

5

If it's all about Customers – make it so

This will not be a long chapter. In fact, it is short but very sweet. It is potentially by far the most profitable chapter of the book. For some, it will be the most profitable chapter of any business book they will ever read. I promise you the next few hundred words can return you at least thousands of times what you have paid for this book – and, if you are spending millions, then it could quite easily return its jacket price a million times over.

This is not a wild or crazy claim. It is quite simply the reward you will get from re-focusing the way you spend your marketing budget based on the information you have already been given in this book. This is, with no word of exaggeration, probably the single largest marketing miracle that you can perform for your business. What you are about to read has, quite literally, enabled me to turn companies round. In one notable case, we achieved massive increases in sales, which almost defied explanation, while simultaneously cutting marketing spending by upwards of 40 per cent. Imagine what that did to the bottom line! And Customers loved it – well, they must have… otherwise it wouldn't have worked.

You don't have to be incredibly clever or skilled to achieve the kind of results I'm talking about – but, on behalf of the business, it does take courage. It takes courage not because I will propose that you take any risks, but simply because people – marketing people or other senior management – *believe* it will involve risk. This is only because they have been doing what they have been doing, and have been accepting that the activities of the past were right or necessary, when really they were neither.

Not so much new as forgotten

You already know what I am about to tell you. There is nothing radically new in it; nothing you don't probably already feel in your heart or accept in your brain. It is simply that the time has come to break the habits of the past and do something different. If there is a difficulty attached to what comes next in this chapter, it is most likely to be to do with persuading and convincing others to come along with you.

I was introduced to one of my favourite sayings during a course of NLP (Neuro-Linguistic Programming). It is this:

> If you go on doing what you've always done,
> You'll go on getting what you've always got.
> If it's not working –
> CHANGE IT!

The only problem with this notion is that it requires us to accept that what we've been doing was not right – or, rather, was not the best way. What makes this harder to handle is that what we have been doing has probably been the accepted practice of your business – and 99 per cent of all other businesses – for decades. It's not just you who are doing it – it is nearly everybody else as well. And we all know that the rest of the world can't be wrong! And yet, almost whatever you read or watch or hear at the moment is giving us all the same message. It's telling us that there is so much rampant change around in every sphere of business that success is less likely to be achieved by doing better what we already do. It is about finding timely ways to approach and tackle our problems and opportunities. Well, this is a timely way – there is no time like the present! Yet, unlike new ways, this thesis has already been tried and tested for us. So, when someone says to me, 'The rest of the world can't be wrong', I answer, 'Yes they can!'

That means all the smart business academics, all the textbooks, all the writers and theorists, all the fancy international advertising agencies, and, for many years, me – we have all been wrong! The only people who might have got this right were probably the same people we talked about at the very beginning of this book. The one-man bands, the craftsmen and women who weren't doing it because it made sense, but were doing it instinctively. As I said earlier, the bigger we get, the harder we seem to make life for ourselves. And the more we do, the more we seem to seek outside help or advice, and the more we seem to think, somehow, that someone must know better than we do ourselves. Well, the fact is that they don't, as the Focus Game demonstrates.

The following is absurdly sensible. It just recognizes the facts of sales and marketing life and experience.

Grab your courage – this could make you a fortune. Or, perhaps, shift your career up several notches. All you have to do is follow these guidelines…and convince the others that you're right. And sane!

The Focus Game

Often, when I am invited into a new business for the first time I will sit with a marketing, sales or managing director and invite them to play the Focus Game.

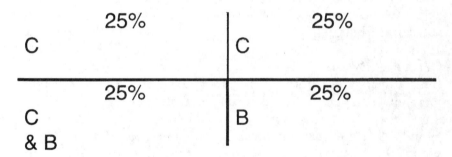

Figure 5.1 The Focus Game – Part One

You can see in Figure 5.1 a cross with '25 per cent' in each zone. Underneath each 25 per cent is a missing word with the first letter in place so that you can fill it in. The figures of 25 per cent are for the game only; ignore them when you apply the game to your own situation. They simply allow me to lead you through a short series of thought processes, which are designed to get you to think about how and why we spend our marketing money at present and what the effects might be if we spent it differently. It is, on paper, just a game. But when you apply the thoughts it provokes, you will save marketing money on the one hand and radically increase your marketing productivity on the other. I cannot promise the proportions, but I can promise the effect, as long as it is done well. The combined effect is a miracle.

OK, here we go. In connection with the first (top left) zone, the word is 'Customer'. And my question is this: 'Do you spend more than 25 per cent of your total marketing spend on your existing Customers?' Invariably, the answer is 'No'. Well, why not? Global experience indicates that you will get 5–15 times more effectiveness from money spent on existing Customers than from money spent on 'cold' activity, and it is plainly crazy to spend most of your money where it will achieve the least.

In the top right zone, the missing word is 'conquest'. My question is: 'Do you spend more than 25 per cent of your total marketing spend on conquest or prospecting or new business activity?' Invariably the answer is 'yes' and, again, my response is – why? For heavens sake, if our experience matches even the worst of the rest of the world, then by shifting, say, 10 per cent of our budget from this to spending it wisely on Customers, we would experience the equivalent of tripling the Customer budget.

Of course, this is where the big boys who frequent the peak TV slots chip in with questions like, 'But what about awareness?' or, 'But what about brand building?' To which I ask why the two activities of prospect or conquest and Customer communications can't deliver brand effects. Of course they can – as you will read later in this chapter in the Marie Curie Cancer Care story. In fact, they do! Moreover, we can pump them up to make sure they do even better than ever before. Which is why the words missing from the lower left zone are 'corporate' and 'brand'. And the question which accompanies this zone is: 'Do you spend more than 25 per cent of your total marketing budget on corporate or brand issues?' Again, the answer is always a whomping convincing 'yes'. Yet again, I have to ask 'why?'. I can tell you the answer.

Your business, in common with around 95 per cent of other businesses, is running the bath with the plug out. All I am suggesting is that you put the plug in. All I want to do is get rid of profligate proportions of waste and really focus your marketing resources where they will do the most good. Most businesses are chasing round spending an unnecessary fortune on new business acquisition when they are sitting on a wealth of untapped business that is locked up in their own existing Customer base. If you release this, not only do you put on business, but you do so at an incredibly low cost in comparison with completely new acquisition, which is probably one of the most expensive things any business can do.

Instead of complacently neglecting old and new Customers alike and misguidedly setting off for more prospecting and more acquisition, we need to start the process of engendering growth, creating a bond, building a relationship, satisfying all the needs and building loyalty. And we need to go on doing that for as long as possible. Acquisition should be kept to the bare minimum to meet the business plan.

Oh! Did I forget to tell you what the word is for that fourth zone? It is BANK! For there is nothing else you need to do, nowhere else you need to spend. By re-focusing to make sure that every penny works to its optimum level, you should have improved performance and reduced costs by, theoretically, 25 per cent. In practice, this can be much, much more. So bank the difference!

Now, you may not want to bank the difference. You may have much better ways to deploy your savings – but I ask you, how would your bottom line look next year with 25 per cent of your marketing budget added to it and sales going through the roof?

Let's go round that loop again. Let's look at each of the zones and really get to understand what the simple but rich suggestion is. We'll re-visit this with a little expansion on the theory. We'll take the top two zones first.

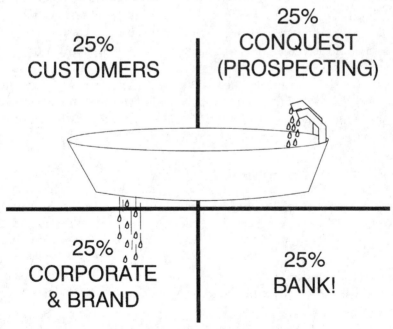

Figure 5.2 The Focus Game – Part Two

While we do that, take a look at the repeated model Figure 5.2 – The Focus Game Part Two – and notice the bath that has been superimposed over the top two zones. You will notice the taps are in the prospecting and new business area and the plug end is in the existing Customer zone. You will also notice that the taps are both full on and the plug is out so that Customers are draining out the other end. This is a really powerful visual image to work with while you are considering this concept. All you have to do to transform your business is to put the metaphorical plug in and then adjust the taps to the level you want. Or, in some cases, you can keep the taps running and pull up a second bath!

What we forgot to remember

Focus your thoughts solely on the top two zones – existing Customers and conquest or prospecting for the next few moments.

Let's get right back to basics. Let me show you something I call the 'Time-Tested Time Test'. It is quite simply one of those experiences or 'knowings' that has been handed down to salespeople almost since selling began. In this form it is applicable to financial consumer markets but actually, if anything, it applies equally or perhaps even more to most other consumer, professional and business markets, and anyone can adapt it to their own situation. It is basically a list, in descending order, of the most effective places you can spend your time if you want to end up with a big fat order book. To salespeople this is one of those crazy things that we all know is right, but we have enormous trouble switching off that damn machine that seems to have been built in to us. That machine instructs us to seek out totally new Customers, and teaches us that a wealth of new Customers is some kind of Holy Grail for which we should strive.

Of course, nothing could be further from the truth. Direct marketers proved it when they experienced those massive differences in response and cost effectiveness between their own Customer lists and those 'cold' lists they rented in. Salespeople have experienced this across time and there are even jokes about the infamous drudge of cold calling. Look at the list below from a higher level. This reminds professional marketers that the further away we get from existing Customers, the less fertile the ground gets, and the harder it is to make sales.

The Time-Tested Time Test

1. Visit and review existing Customers;
2. other visits to existing Customers (courtesy and service calls);
3. family referrals;
4. other referrals;
5. orphans (Customers currently unassigned to salespeople or intermediaries);
6. lapsed Customers;
7. other corporate leads and promotions;
8. 'cold' activities.

As I said, this list was used by sales managers to help their salespeople evaluate the focus or investment of their time and effort. Notice that it is only when we reach items 7 and 8 that we begin to step beyond the influence of Customers.

This is your rationale for re-focusing budget into those areas. That money moves across the model from the 'tap' side to the 'plug' side and, if achieved well, starts to put the plug in by increasing your share of the Customer spend. This leads to an increase in sales and a decrease in Customer attrition simultaneously. Now, and it can be quite suddenly, you find your costs decreasing and your business targets more easily achieved. Indeed, you are in the luxurious position of adjusting the taps to decide just how much new business you really want. In many ways, I am as much concerned about 'share of Customer' as I am about share of market.

Share of Customer or share of spend is so much more revealing about how a business is succeeding in the soft issues of Customer relationships – in other words, it is a handy measure of the solidity and value of what it is doing on the 'plug' side. Incidentally, while share of Customer is a notoriously difficult thing to measure, it is also a powerful tool when used as a key performance indicator by sales management.

Now for the brand and corporate issues: Zone Three

To return to the second circuit of the model, and to reflect upon the brand zone, it would be foolish to believe that brand, corporate or product work would ever be totally unnecessary because your Customer and prospecting activities were so brand-conscious and so brand-powerful. However, there is a strong case that money should in most cases be fairly drastically reduced in this area. Awareness and recall do not in themselves reveal precise information that reliably relates to sales. The power of what we might, for want of better words, still describe as the 'mass media' – by which I mean the media that cover slabs of our market *en masse* – can affect both existing and prospective Customers. The question really is how much more you can achieve when you strap brand work to other Customer or prospecting activity or communications. And the answer is that you can achieve miracles! Some of this money is usually, therefore, channelled into the marketing effort in the top two zones of the model. Some slides sideways and becomes an element of the cost savings.

Many of the so-called below-the-line media have come to realize that they can play a much greater role in both the brand- and corporate-building process. Thus, whereas once they concentrated solely on their tactical objectives, they now spread across both planes – tactics and strategy. This duality of role makes good economic sense. And it makes powerful advertising too.

The Marie Curie story

I learned this lesson from my late father Thomas Bernard Robinson OBE, who founded the Marie Curie Memorial Foundation, more popularly recognized these days as Marie Curie Cancer Care. It's a somewhat romantic story, starting with the influence of Sir Winston Churchill, to whom my father directly reported towards the end of the Second World War. An old lady, hearing of his intention to start a cancer charity, took off her engagement ring and offered it to him. He sold it, as she had suggested, for about £75.

In those days, £75 was a reasonable sum for a first donation; my father decided to devote all of it to raising more money. He sent out a mailing (although I suspect his early efforts of hand-picked, hand-signed missives didn't seem like direct mail to him!) to raise funds. It was successful. The amassed funds financed another mailing, and so on, until he had built a base of regular subscribers and enough surplus to start on the serious work of fighting cancer and caring for the stricken.

As the years passed, professional marketing skills increased and my father learned, as all charities do, that the donor base becomes the high-response, high-donation centre of activity, and the prospecting element is the low-response, low-donation part. Indeed, it is quite often only the lifetime value of a donor that makes the prospecting effort worthwhile. I wonder why people expect marketing a charity to be any different from other businesses! Many have found that one acquires a donor at a loss, which is turned into profit later through re-approaches and, perhaps, by trading in some way.

As more years passed, my father became more creative. He introduced a mailing shot that covered ten houses at once (and effectively blackmailed each house into giving more than the last!); he found a way to personalize mailings before personalization was economically viable, thus for many years turning the telephone books into his top-pulling list; as well as – may we all forgive him – the Charity Christmas Seal.

By now, the Marie Curie was mailing its donor list (the word database had not been invented) twice a year, and 'cold' prospects mailings were despatched in millions. Literally. At one point, I believe, the rate was well in excess of 12 million a year; for one extensive period, this was more than any other charity, and for almost two decades he mailed more than any other cancer charity.

There were two side-effects, both extremely valuable. Both, all these years later, hold a moral for all advertisers, especially those who use direct marketing.

Moral One

My father accrued extraordinary loyalty from his regular donors, to the point where massive levels of legacy income were attributable to the long-term donors. Indeed, in the fundraising world, the correlation between loyalty building through long-term donor mailings and legacy income is now widely recognized.

Moral Two

Marie Curie achieved the No. 1 slot in brand awareness. Their unprompted figures left the others light years behind! The lesson here is that this coveted position was achieved without spending any significant sums on advertising. The 'advertising effect' was achieved as a by-product of the massive mailings. It cost my father nothing.

The Marie Curie example clearly demonstrates what many advertising traditionalists have been reluctant to admit. Direct mail, like many of the other marketing disciplines, can have a powerful effect on brand building and brand equity, and make an equally strong contribution to the process of loyalty building, which, as the marketing world re-focuses on relationships, will be thrown increasingly into the spotlight. Indeed, since writing *Total Quality Marketing*, I have come to believe this to be the single most important success leverage factor for marketing in the years ahead. This is why this book has a chapter that will enable you to understand and manage loyalty building. It's truly wonderful miracle territory, I promise you. Nothing is more certain, when it comes to loyalty building, than this book's title – 'It's all about Customers'.

In this chapter we have discovered a rationale that can be quite quickly adopted to make us question how and why our marketing investment is deployed. With intelligent re-focusing, marketing budgets can be made to work much, much harder. This is done by finding new and different answers to the following questions:

- Why do we spend so little of the total of our marketing cash and resource on existing Customers when time-honoured wisdom and many decades of experience by direct and other marketers indicate that spending more on existing Customers guarantees significantly higher returns?
- Why do we spend so much of our marketing money and effort on finding new business when everyone accepts that prospecting and conquest business is the hardest and most expensive thing we can do?
- Why do we not achieve significant brand building through all our Customer and prospecting activity and communications when these can achieve so much, to such great effect, for so little cost?

6

How to develop ISMS

Integrated sales, marketing and service (ISMS) is 'the seamless delivery of sales, marketing and service to the Customer in complete harmony with the relationship and in real time'.

One of my Clients, after much debate, came to this definition: 'Integrated marketing means achieving synergistic effects between different means of communication through integration of goals, messages, execution and timing. The goal is to create a long-term relationship with Customers through a mutually productive and profitable dialogue. Each activity also has a short-term measurable goal. Goal fulfilment is always measured in an organized way.'

That definition is somewhat more explicit and pragmatic than mine and leads to the following answers to the question 'What is ISMS?'

- Using sales, advertising, telephone and mail in the right mix;
- integration of marketing activities with service activities for improved synergy;
- using a marketing database for managing the activity.

Next, we set about identifying the stepping stones to achieving those three objectives. The list that follows is authentic and was created from a project definition gathering – and, as such, is in no particular priority, includes a few peripheral issues and puts the numbers last. I have not included it because it is definitive or prescriptive. I have included it because it is typical. Indeed, it would not do for any other business because every starting point is unique. Just as yours will be. And their destination was unique, just as yours will be.

The following projects or activities emerged:

1. create one single Customer database;
2. clean up the database;
3. categorize and grade Customers;
4. resolve how to handle actual versus potential sales;
5. improve telesales facilities and capabilities;
6. install the new database system in all countries;
7. find and include *all* relevant Customer information on database;
8. set up continuous Customer satisfaction procedures including measurement and analysis;
9. devise accurate measurement processes to analyse cost/results of marketing activities;
10. define *all* Customer activities and communications and audit to uncover improvement areas;
11. co-ordinate all (sales and) marketing and service activities by Customer;
12. agree the uses of existing data and needs for new data;
13. educate and train the sales, marketing and Customer service teams;
14. involve the above in the creation and development of ISMS;
15. take very seriously information from the salesforce about Customers: find ways to encourage the information flow;
16. decide how best to use the above information wisely to enhance Customer relationships;
17. make Customers aware of ISMS and enable them to feel the benefits as quickly as possible;
18. encourage sales and service teams to take a 'room for improvement' attitude to complaints or potential complaints;
19. improve complaint handling and response times;
20. install a new bonus system across the business that is related to and reflects upward and downward movement of Customer satisfaction and loyalty;
21. gain the total commitment of the whole organization;
22. encourage advice for service improvements from the whole company;
23. create and maintain the spirit for and excitement about ISMS;
24. Customer loyalty: identify the key performance indicators and develop the monitoring and measurement systems.

Integrated Clients, definitely. But what is an integrated agency?

Leaving aside my suggestion for replacing integrated marketing with the wider-ranging notion of ISMS for a moment, there is much confusion. Integrated marketing appears to mean very different things to different people. I have worked internally with a number of Clients and facilitated meetings to determine their definition of integrated marketing. With each group we come to definitions that, if taken to one of the other businesses, would not fit at all. Thus, I believe integrated marketing to be a custom-built solution for your business. It is a series of processes designed specifically to fit your advertising, sales, marketing and – for ISMS – service objectives and deliver them to your market. The result is relationship marketing.

This already uncovers one of the fallacies about integrated marketing. How can agencies, predominantly ex (and not so ex!) direct marketing agencies, call themselves integrated marketing agencies? Integrated marketing is not something an agency can supply – it is a business function. True, a few agencies can supply those who are using integrated marketing techniques. When they work with a company using integrated marketing, they are being asked to have a strategic understanding of how marketing works in a business that communicates with its market in an integrated fashion. This means that the agency must be capable of all the usual functions and certainly should be well equipped with 'direct' communication skills, which are essential to integration. However, the agency must also be able to administrate for, and cope with, a vast diversity of much smaller – in size and budget – tasks. The 'integrated' Client uses very narrowcast communications. Such a Client will be endeavouring to transmit as many of its communications and messages to enhance, as nearly as possible, one-to-one Customer relationships and will inevitably be using some method of communications management.

To be quite clear, integrated marketing does not simply mean sales, advertising and marketing activity all fitting together very neatly. Integrated marketing is business activity of any kind that has integrity with Customer relationships and encompasses the service aspect of the Customer relationship. These activities and messages are inseparably bound together with the Customer relationship – *they make sense to that Customer*.

When 'it all fits together' – even if it all fits together very well – then we have good campaign planning. If the ads on TV support the mailing and the retail activity, which harmonizes with the point-of-sale materials, which tie in with the sales presenters, and the salespeople give out the same message, that's admirable. If many Customers buy, and find that everything that was said was true and they are happy, then you had a good campaign. It all fitted together. What I have just described is not integrated marketing, it is simply an example of an effective and well-planned campaign. It is not a new idea, but has been around for years. What is missing is any connection to the nature and state of the Customer relationship.

One-to-one can be a state of mind, a way of life

All Customers deserve ISMS as a state of mind; not all of them will get it as a way of life. Indeed, not all of them want or expect it as a way of life.

If I am a casual buyer of your brand of toothpaste, perhaps I buy it when it's on special offer; my demand is basically limited to the product. You can do things to change that, but you have an uphill climb because I'm a price-shopper. If, on the other hand, I buy your toothpaste regularly, I'm brand loyal, and I demonstrate the desire to be so, potentially for life (or as long as I have teeth!), I have a different perception or expectation of you. You are more important to me and I am hugely more important to you. You should know who I am and I should feel that I can talk to you and that you want to hear from me. Equally, I may buy other products from you – different brands – and actually, the sum total of my commitment to your business, even if it is made up of a great number of individual purchases, may have the potential to be quite substantial. I am, to a degree, corporately quite a fan of yours. With conventional marketing I'm a no-name. With Customer-driven marketing, I am someone special. And I know it and appreciate it.

A primary part of the task here is to develop mechanisms that identify and grade your Customers against their expectation and their value or potential value to the business.

Given the opportunity to communicate, share their feelings or voice an opinion, Customers with a higher loyalty potential often identify themselves. They respond to you and, in effect, say, 'Here I am. Listen to me. Speak to me. Recognize me.'

I have a Client whose marketing budget runs into tens of millions of pounds. They have a clientele some of whom could spend as much with them in turnover as that marketing budget. Equally, some may not spend more than £1,000 a year with them. How should this Client deploy ISMS? Are they expected to deal with small spenders in exactly the same way as those businesses which spend tens of millions with them? Plainly, they are not. Even if they were crazy enough to want to, they simply could not afford to.

Customers need to be graded

I have seen businesses grade Customers by turnover, volume offtake (which I don't recommend), and by profit, actual and potential. The grades then need to be matched to a set of Customer service and delivery levels that exceed Customer expectations, while being profitable to you. If this sounds like something of a balancing act, that's fair enough, because that is exactly what it is! It will help, too, if the grading process has direct links to the performance indicators that you will have built into your definition of loyalty, as outlined in 'The nine steps to managing loyalty' in Chapter 4. These common performance measures can also link on through to your motivation and remuneration ideas (for more on this, see Chapter 9). The point, to be clear, is that your performance indicators for loyalty directly link to your measurement and analysis, to your grading system and on to your employee rewards. This ensures cohesion of all the factors.

Customers can go down as well as up!

Much to the upset of some Customer-facing staff, this grading process has a hard edge. The only way is not up! Customers can be downgraded as well as upgraded. They may need sensitive handling when service levels decrease, and competitive service positioning should be watched to ensure that you are not withdrawing something that a competitor would be prepared to give. On the happier side, the desired direction is up, which means increasing the service levels and maintaining them when it tops out. To be quite explicit about this, I am proposing variances in the level of service here, not the standards. The business should only have one set of service standards. It is very slippery ground indeed for an organization to run more than one set.

I said that downgrading can upset Customer-facing staff. It's simply that downgrading is obviously arduous and an unpleasant thing to do – rather like asking a salesperson to collect a late-payment cheque from a Customer. Many would rather leave the debt-chasing to the accounts department! However, the company does not have a bottomless purse and it should be appreciated that those who get too much service deny others their fair share.

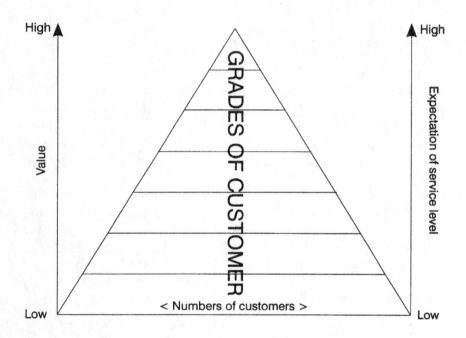

Figure 6.1 The pyramid of expectation. As Customer value increases so does their expectation of service. Customers can be graded by actual and/or potential sales or profit contribution

Some of those Customers, depending on their grade, will expect and understand that they will be spoken to *en masse* via television or the press. Others will demand to be 'account managed', or given personal attention. Each grade should have clearly set out levels of each of the five strands of loyalty – price, product, delivery, service and recognition – and provide the availability to those as far down the pyramid of expectation as possible. The challenge is to exceed Customer expectations at all levels, profitably. Cost-to-serve is an important issue here.

When you come to considering the levels of service and the cost of those activities, remember that your general direction is upwards. We are looking to increase sales from existing Customers – thus, if you are going to err, do so on the generous side! And this is where some assessment or knowledge of Customer potential is helpful. Preferably, this grading process should be carried out for each individual Customer. If your business is a large one, with many Customers, you may decide that your base level precludes much or any individualization. It is precisely at this level that one-to-one becomes philosophical rather than actual. And it is here that I take issue with those who talk about a one-to-one future. It will exist for some – but only if they, or, rather, the relationship, merits it!

So who is trying to have a relationship with whom?

Bags of salt! Regular old table salt. I have vowed to be totally loyal to the brand. I might buy perhaps 50 bags in my whole life. Total value: next to nothing. Service expectation: none. Relationship expectation: none. So does that mean that companies selling salt cannot use ISMS? In my view it does; the only person who has a chance with salt is the retailer, who can lock me in to a major portion of my household spend. So what about the salt company? Well, they are anxious to secure the business of the wholesalers and retailers who buy from them and, yes, ISMS is perfect in that sphere. The wholesalers and retailers, unlike me, both merit and will welcome the full benefits of a Customer-driven business approach.

It's about to get a whole dimension more complicated

The whole puzzle now goes into another dimension, in which we look at the various patterns of purchasing and contact that operate within your business. For, just to complicate things, some Customers wander in and out of full service requirements.

Take an estate agent, for example. Do we really want or expect the agent to keep actively trying to satisfy us right throughout the ten years we might live at a house before we move on again? I hope not. If all our suppliers did this, we wouldn't be able to get to our doors for mail, or have any time for personal telephone calls. We would have come to grief in a communications traffic jam.

I would argue that it would be prudent for the estate agent to stay in touch, to keep us informed of their value to us. Hardly any of them do. They seem to expect that any loyalty they created in one transaction is automatically retained until the next. Of course, it rarely is!

So, with some Customers, the expectation increases around a need or desire. Again, this would affect, for example, a car purchaser or someone who had just acquired a new dishwasher. There is little point generally in sending me details of a new model days after I have purchased another, different one. However, awareness of the new model as part of a Customer contact programme is both sensible and appropriate. A Customer-driven approach would enable the car dealer to know when one family has two of the same make and, for that matter, the dishwasher vendor or manufacturer to know when a household has washing machines, dryers and other devices of the same brand.

What has all this Customer service grading to do with ISMS?

Good question! A lot. I described ISMS earlier as 'the seamless delivery of sales, marketing and service to the Customer'. The three, currently differentiated functions of the business – sales, marketing and service – have to become welded together. How can you possibly weld service into sales and marketing if you don't have some notion of the service levels this has to include? Answer: you can't. However, now that you have decided your service levels, you can start looking at how you deliver the service, how you integrate the functions and how you wish to make those all-important sales to the Customer. You can start to determine and take feedback from Customers on frequency, method and style of contact. This adds to the value balance in line with that Customer's needs and expectations, and brings order and reason to the communications within the relationship. This is why Customer decision making has to move to the front line, along with marketing and the database.

It is also why Customers need to be aligned with, and kept in touch with the individuals who are responsible for them, and why communications must be, or be seen to be, channelled through those same personnel. And the more consistency there is of those personnel, generally, the better chance you have of building corporate and brand relationships. This alignment, without the integration, is perceived by Customers to be shallow and inconsequential. It denies what is happening between them and those claiming to look after or service them. It equally denies your staff the opportunity to take responsibility for Customers, and to do the job required by a Customer-driven business.

The responsibility to which I refer does not relate only to Customers. These people also have a responsibility to increase sales, deliver profit and protect margins by adding value. However, the Customer-driven environment tends to create an atmosphere in which people approach you to buy. This contrasts dramatically with what we have suffered through the previous decades when we studiously made things far tougher and more expensive for ourselves as we went off-track down the route of high-activity marketing.

New tasks, new divisions of labour

In essence, the communications that we have to manage can only fall into two broad categories: inbound and outbound. Inbound communications are relatively easy to manage, since they will generally be through a limited – or limitable – number of media. Typically, for many businesses these will still be written (letters, faxes and e-mail), by telephone or from face-to-face contact. Outbound is more complex, because the choice of media is much wider. The more you move from individual messages, the harder it is to operate in real time for so many relationships, and the more the classic media choices stand winking enticingly at you. To some extent, your choice of media will now be much more affected by the nature of the message. Is it more appropriate to use one of the narrowcast set of choices, or the broadcast? (To be clear, one-to-one is the ultimate narrowcast!) An enormous number of communications are already despatched in thousands to Customers, and many are missing the opportunity to consolidate the relationships between individuals. Why do personalized mailings go out to Customers signed by anyone else other than the front-line person who usually deals with them?

We have to ensure that three vital activities can take place: we need to hear what people have or want to say; we need to be able to respond when they want; and we also need to speak to them from time to time. By 'speak' and 'hear', I mean the use of any communications medium, from individual face-to-face to broadcast television.

The critical issue is that what remains to be done *en masse* does not usurp what is happening at the front line.

How to weld sales, service and marketing together

People who are effective at selling must remain doing what they do best. And the same applies to the service and marketing people. However, structure is important. The task of ISMS needs the welding. And the welding of the three disciplines is achieved by three basic steps.

First – and this is the main priority – people must be aligned with their responsibilities. Their responsibility is clear: to build loyalty through their relationships with Customers. The key issue is Customer relationships. They must be managed and developed by those who will do the work. So don't sit salespeople with salespeople and service people with service people and hope they get the Customer task right. Sit salespeople with service people with marketing people, and charge them with looking after the same group of Customers together. Then the task, the goals and the alignment are in harmony with your real objective, which is your first priority. This is explained in the granular business concept in Chapter 9.

The next priority is to make sure that the front-line staff have the information to do the job. The database is a critical factor. If any one of the three functions cannot access Customer information that is both accurate and up to date, they cannot possibly succeed. They must also, then, take responsibility for the data quality. Now we are beginning to have integration!

Lastly, let them work out their own responsibilities and demarcation lines. The important thing is their commitment and dedication to the Customer. That is all.

The final words go to Customer communications

I have placed the view before you that, as communications become more narrowcast, then the management of them must also move as near the front line as possible. However, there is no point in it doing so unless they add relevance and timing to it. For example, front-line people should be able to de-select Customers from, say a mailing, on the basis that they think it would be better to call the Customer first and tell them about it, and then perhaps follow up with further information (based on the Customer's choice) through the post or by visit. As long as they are adding relevance, power and timing to the message, it is up to them whether it works. It's their responsibility. It's not hard. They just have to remember one central thought. It's all about Customers.

In this chapter we have seen that ISMS is as individual to your business as the results of it are to your Customer relationships. In summary, this means the following.

- Integrated sales marketing and service (ISMS) welds the sales, marketing and service functions together to provide seamless delivery of the corporate promise to the Customer in complete harmony with the Customer relationship and in real time.
- ISMS is a custom-built solution for your business. It should be designed specifically to fit your Customer-driven business needs. The objective is to deliver relationship marketing.
- ISMS should not be confused with effective campaign planning. This notion is as old as the hills – and very effective! The true concept of ISMS is one that brings order, sense and relevance to the communications and interactions as judged against individual Customer relationships.
- One-to-one can be a state of mind – a goal to aim at, a philosophical desire – for some and an actuality for others. Not all Customers merit one-to-one treatment and not all expect it.
- Performance indicators for loyalty should be embedded in your definition of loyalty directly linked to measurement and analysis, to the grading system and on to employee rewards. This ensures cohesion of all the factors.
- Customers have to be graded by turnover or profit, actual and potential. The grades are matched to a set of Customer service and corporate delivery levels, which exceed Customer expectations while being profitable for the business. Customers should be downgraded as well as upgraded. It is important that, whereas service levels may vary, service standards do not.
- Customers' expectation of service increases broadly in line with their spend – or with their value to the business. The task of individualization is to extend the five strands of loyalty – price, product, delivery, service and recognition – as far down the pyramid of expectation as possible. This calculation should have relevance to the cost-to-serve.
- For some businesses, Customers' expectations of service vary, set against their needs or desires.
- The grading of Customers to determine appropriate service levels is important to ISMS. It ensures that when sales, marketing and service are welded together, the levels are understood and commonly worked towards.

- The alignment of staff – not by discipline, but by Customer groups – is critical. They will share Customer objectives but they will also share responsibility for sales, profit and margin protection. It is this structuring that provides the welding of sales, marketing and service.
- Customer communications divide cleanly into inbound and outbound: inbound are comparatively easy to manage because of clear and limited media choice. The nature of the outbound message should have greater influence over media choice. Every effort should be made not to usurp what is happening at the front line. As many communications as possible should be channelled or be seen to be channelled through front-line individuals.
- The Customer database is critical. Therefore the teams of realigned staff must take responsibility for data accuracy and data quality. Within their teams, they should agree their own demarcation lines for work and responsibilities.
- Front-line staff should get as much control as possible over Customer communications, but it is incumbent upon them to add relevance and timing.

7

Managing communications

With all the new technology multiplying with all the new media, we are inevitably heading for a potential communications traffic jam. So many people trying to say so many things, so many different ways, so many times, to increasingly *fewer* (in other words more closely targeted) individuals.

The people I buy from want to communicate with me; the people I used to buy from are ringing and writing and knocking on my door. My fax machine responds to a caller who is trying to get me to be a Customer of theirs. The cellphone interrupts the commercials on the radio, which distract me from the posters telling me which paper I should buy to decide which TV channel I should watch; that's if I have time after I've downloaded my e-mails. I think I'm getting mediaphobia!

But who cares anyway? I can zap the lot of them! Figures published in France show that 'technologically advanced homes' (those where there is a remote-control channel changer) will make changes while the ads are on; 31 per cent will look around the other channels while 29 per cent just kill the sound. The birth of the silent TV ad is just around the corner. When you've got it, you simply show it on all channels simultaneously. Easy!

Seriously, I am quite convinced that this 'traffic jam' will become one of the most critical factors for marketers of the future. Why? Because it is the crossroads for so many of the other factors: communications, the media explosion, the techno-splosion, the desire to improve Customer service, and so on, and ever on. The Romans were quite prophetic when they came up with the word 'trivia'. Apparently, it is derived from the Latin for 'three roads'. In Roman times, they decided that, wherever three roads met, there was likely to be enough traffic to merit a bulletin board. Hence the word. Even the communications traffic jam is not new! And poster site contractors already know this.

To fan the flames of this burning issue, there is a common fallacy among marketers that more communication equals better service and, equally, that better service means more communication. It may be true in some cases, but one is not a prerequisite of the other. I will, however, concede that very often more communication *feels* like better service.

I am no friend of the phrase 'junk mail'; many people who are Customers of some of the more old-fashioned direct marketing or mail order houses still suffer from a seemingly endless bombardment of apparently untargeted mail that invades their letterbox. I doubt that any of these Customers would agree that more communication equals better service.

I carried out a fascinating exercise just recently for one large mailer. This large insurance company was well and truly locked in to the old way of direct marketing. They still saw it as a numbers game. They hammered the house file without any thought to profiling, segmentation, or any real targeting. There was no consideration of the damage that over-mailing or irrelevant mailing might do to business but, simply, an obsession with the old notion that, the bigger the run, the lower the unit cost and, therefore, the lower the breakeven. With this product and this highly aggressive and incentivized mailing pack the breakeven was a tiny 0.4 per cent. Easy! Chuck it in the mail!

I started working on the difference in lifetime values of business brought in by mailings like this as opposed to other more sensitively prepared and targeted approaches. These projected clear corporate and brand values but, most of all, were in harmony with the Customer or prospect information.

Instead of measuring business written at the front end, I started examining damage down the back end in terms of Customer opinions, attitudes, satisfaction, performance and loyalty. I was able to demonstrate quite conclusively that the huge, untargeted, over-promotional mailings were actually doing more damage than anything else, in low-profit, low-persistency business at the front end. For certain this is completely off-track for marketing miracle seekers.

In fact, the kind of direct mail I am describing was born and grew up in the USA, and has been cloned around the world. On a recent trip to Asia, Manila Bankers Life brought along just such a mailing to a seminar I was doing. I think these mailings must have been invented long before the phrase 'brand equity' was born. They were workhorse mailings: they cost little, pulled low, but were unassailably cost-effective. They were – are – junk mail! Just as throwing leaflets out of a plane is principally litter!

These mailings are still quite common in the USA, and this may be contributing to the way the reputation and reception for direct marketing is nose-diving there compared with Europe, where it seems to be predominantly either on a level, or slightly improving. For example, the USA, which has historically enjoyed a reputation of being one of the more 'friendly' countries towards direct mail, has seen figures for that friendliness reduce over recent years as follows: 1987 – 68 per cent; 1990 – 57 per cent; 1993 – 46 per cent. In 1994, it was calculated that 44 per cent of US direct mail was thrown away unread or unopened. In the UK recently, 77 per cent of direct mail *users* claimed that the quality of direct mail was improving. I agree with this and believe it to be because of the increasing recognition that direct marketing techniques can be powerful brand builders as well as powerful business builders.

However, you can actually turn this issue the other way round and know you are on safe ground. That's to say we can be quite sure that bad or lower-quality communications will damage (or be perceived by the Customer to threaten) Customer relationships. The need therefore is to focus on, assess and prioritize the quality, method and validity of the communications. To over-communicate or to mis-communicate generally will actually harm Customer relationships. Nothing gives Customers a more telling idea of how much a company cares for them than the organization of its communications.

You may have experienced the appalling frustration of ringing someone with an enquiry or complaint and being passed around a building from extension to extension, each time repeating your story to someone who doesn't know you from 2 million Customers. This is not a question of bad company organization or structure. It is not a question necessarily of poorly trained or motivated staff. It is usually the sign of a company that doesn't appreciate that Customer service starts with having someone you know will be there. You know they know you. You know they will sort things out. You know they know what's going on in relation to you. *They* care about *you*. A miracle in itself!

An example that springs to mind is that of call handling and call centres. For one Client we organized some research among its

Customers and non-Customers. By massive amounts Customers told us how they positively loathe all the latest telephone automation; top of the bill of hatred was 'relentless tiers of option menus' and 'recorded solutions or information'. As a result, we made massive changes to the call-centre organization. Customers with a problem had clear ideas of what they wanted. First, they wanted a human being. Second, they wanted that human being as quickly as possible (according to the research, 30 seconds was considered a long time). Third, they wanted 'ownership' of the problem or query by the person taking the call. Fourth, they wanted immediate or near-immediate action. Fifth, they wanted – in this order – responsibility, honesty and courtesy.

Our solution led to some interesting side effects. Our goal was to provide 'a capable, responsible, courteous human being [who] will be listening to you within 15 seconds'. Very early on, during the project definition stage, it became clear that we were going to have to break some conventions in order to achieve our result. It was decided that we would discard some fairly seriously expensive kit brought in from the USA. It was also decided that the theme would be 'power to the people'. In this case, the 'people' were those in the call-centre teams.

Now, for example, if you ring with a product information request, here's what happens. Within 15 seconds, you get a pleasant, well-trained person to listen to you. The same pleasant, well-trained person then plays back to you what they have heard and what they will do and by when. That same person then gets out of their seat, goes to the stationery cupboard, puts the selection of product information together. They put it in an envelope with a personally signed compliment slip or letter. They put it in the mail tray. And then they ring you back to confirm they have dealt with the matter and to leave a personal re-contact number so you can reach them personally, if required. Consistency of contact is always a high priority with Customers. And a real feather in your cap if you can achieve it. It featured in the five strands of loyalty under the heading of 'recognition'.

Just before we move on, it would be worth mentioning some of the unexpected side effects that followed. First, productivity was not as damaged as we thought it might be. This was contributed to by much higher energy, motivation and commitment from the operatives. A social environment developed as operators left their desks to attend to Customer needs and problems. This cut operator churn by almost half. Further, personnel felt liked and appreciated by both Customers and their own management. They enjoyed the responsibility, and not feeling (I quote directly) 'like a bunch of battery hens with headsets'. What's more, since these things together cut staff losses so dramatically, there were very pleasant side effects in terms of both recruitment and training costs.

Customers – consumer or business – also need to be someone

Like the majority of people in the UK, I bank with one of the major high street banks, which tell their Customers that they have a 'personal banker'. My personal banker doesn't know me. My personal banker is strangely absent when things go wrong. To him I am a number rather than a name. When things go wrong, the manager signs a form letter, which was written either by a manager at the same branch in 1956 and has served well ever since, or which was possibly written by the corporate form-letter writing officer.

It seems to me that this simple basic human financial need – a banking service – cries out for a number of things:

● to be made more human, not less so;
● more recognition, knowledge and understanding;
● to be of optimum benefit to the Customer, whether delivered at a distance or not.

None of this defies automation; rather, it requires it. Surely there must be a miracle or two waiting to be discovered here?

It is the use to which the automation is put that must change. Why was it possible in the 1950s, but, with all the technology and communications at our disposal in the 1990s, is apparently neither available, achievable nor cost-effective?

I had an extraordinary conversation with one bank's branch manager one day. I asked him how many staff he employed. Having explained to me, at first, that this was highly confidential information, he finally agreed to let me in on the fact he had, say, 25.

Next question. How many individual banking Customers did he have? Well, he couldn't possibly let me know that, I was being quite absurd. Finally, after the most extraordinary game playing, I was allowed to come to a conclusion that he felt would not 'mislead' me. For the sake of the story and round figures, let's say this was 5,000.

Thanking him for this help I asked him whether – in theory only, just as a hypothesis, mind – it would be possible to distribute the 5,000 Customers among the 25 staff so that each had 200 to look after. The man was outraged. Some only had this skill, some only had that training. Who would answer the phones and take care of 'housekeeping'? Was I, with respect, completely mad?

I tried again. OK, what if we put five people on one side to do all those non-Customer things, was it possible then to divide the Customers among the staff so that each of the 20 remaining staff had 250 Customers? He checked again. This was a hypothesis? Yes. He was only answering theoretically speaking – because I did understand there would be enormous problems of technical competence, and so on? Yes, I did understand. Then, reluctantly, he admitted that yes, it was possible. But why was I asking?

Because, as I explained, *this* would feel to me like personal banking. I would get to know the banker, they would get to know me. I could begin to feel 'looked after' because they would indeed be looking after me – personally. It would, indeed, merit the word 'personal'. A miracle if ever there was!

Now he understood. Why hadn't I explained in the first place? Moreover, the bank did have some places where this actually already happened, where genuine personal banking was really given. I was surprised. Where? How? For whom?

It transpired that you needed a minimum of £100,000 with the bank to merit the service.

Yes, why do more Customers mean less service?

It is another fallacy to believe that Customer service has to decline with the number of Customers being dealt with. Yet, in banking and many other services, automation and technology should have provided these suppliers with the means to maintain quality while profitably delivering service. It appears not to have done so.

So here is a classic Customer service dilemma, one that many organizations would set about solving, just as some have, by providing someone (or two!) who will speak to you personally, who can call up your information on their screen, who can pretend to know you. Your 'personal banker'. And so they are. Just as soon as you tell them your account number!

My Customer number should be number 1 – and so should all the others

Oddly enough, the bank example is only a fraction away from the right answer. It's just that they should provide the service, not just lip service. I have dwelt on this example not because I have the answer but because marketers need to consider how the problem is solved. To their credit, some banks have managed to avoid the obvious mistake – the campaign answer.

This is one of marketing's favourite solutions – to hit the problem head on with a campaign to prove to the Customer that no problem really exists. A campaign is mounted to make personalities of the various service managers at the bank, to hold 'open evenings' so that you can meet all your 'friends' at the branch (they're the ones who still need to give you a name badge!). And so on. Psychologists maintain that people often say the exact opposite of what they feel, want, or believe – this campaign is a classic example of the syndrome. Now you are encouraged to communicate with each individual 'expert' for each service. And, of course, they will do the same. You'll get letters from the insurance experts, phone calls from their investment experts, and the mandatory quarterly newsletter or magazine. You now have a standard Customer service campaign formula at work on you. No miracles there!

How does it feel to be just another Customer, Mr Whatsyername?

You're about to enjoy the communications traffic jam. Junk mail from head office. More from the branch. Telephone calls when you least want them. And that's happening with almost every business you use: your bank, your insurance company, your travel agent or holiday company, all your credit card companies, and the department store, catalogue, and so on.

Hang on to your hats. In the next ten years, you'll see these messages come from your personal fax, your e-mail system, your video phone (tellyphone) or wall, not to mention the PC link you have and, of course, your interactive television. Super-clean digital satellite transmissions or hi-tech fibre-optic lines will bring all this to your home – all of which will offer you virtual and tele-shopping and the latest in video mail order catalogues. So alongside e-commerce, you'll have an interactive entertainment and communication system. You see why there could be a traffic jam!

Who loves ya, baby?

So who loves you? Is it the people who communicate the most, or the people who manage their communications best who build a successful relationship with you? The difference will be that the latter have a Total Communications Management (TCM) policy – one person (or one small team of people) looks after you, understands your dealings and knows you. It happened in the 1950s and now, thanks to our technology revolutions and, particularly, to the capabilities of sophisticated marketing databases and intelligent internal company communications, it can happen again. We can definitely find miracles here.

I have worked with one small family bank where we have adapted the entry security system to help deliver better Customer service. It is in a country where it is quite usual to swipe your account or credit card to open the doors on entry. That's the security bit. Now the Customer service bit. We hooked the door-entry technology up to the bank's computers. Then we placed a large electronic noticeboard at the lobby entry. This advised Customers which teller to visit.

Each time the Customer would be channelled to the same teller, Joanna, for example. If Joanna was away, it would direct the Customer to Terry. Indeed, whenever Joanna was not there, it would always propose Terry. And if Terry wasn't there? Then, the Customer would consistently be recommended to Lynne. Always the same three. If the Customer decided to use the cash machine in the lobby on the way to the teller, that transaction was included in the information that was pumped through to the teller's PC ready for his or her arrival. The information was in, as near as possible, real time. Terrific! But here's what happened…it was a definite miracle.

With this project the chairman had asked me to push the bank back to the days he remembered when, as a child, he used to go there with his father, and they were always greeted by name. That bit was easy. Interestingly, we found that, within months, the technology was almost unnecessary with regular visitors. The tellers and the Customers got to know each other and many were back to the good old days without any of the fancy kit!

When it is used for the right end result, technology is quite wonderful at knocking the clock back, and getting us back to those times when individual, personal, caring service was what everybody got.

TCM brings order out of chaos and someone who recognizes you

The TCM (Total Communications Management) strategy is effective for the individual consumer, the family unit, or any scale of business. The fundamental realization is that the communications are not there to sell in their own right (the cause of junk mail!), but they are the means through which the interaction – the dialogue – of the relationship will take place. There is absolutely no reason why they cannot be made to sell for you. However, to do so effectively, it must be recognized that selling, or repeat or cross-selling, to a Customer within the privileged, trusted position of a Customer care or Customer service programme is a very different activity with a very different tone and a very different style.

Did you notice that word 'trusted'? What impact did it make on you? Does selling to an existing Customer feel like selling from a position of trust? This trust is perhaps most openly and obviously displayed in the way that you organize your communications with the Customer. How can I trust, or give any semblance of credibility to, a 'personal banker' who doesn't know me, doesn't know my name, doesn't know my financial position, and doesn't understand the background of my relationship with the bank? Plainly, I can't. The title exaggerates.

Let's get back to your miracle hunting ground. What do I mean when I suggest and repeat that the organization of the communications is the shaft of realization through which Customers will most quickly assess the true level of caring that goes on for them within any organization? Simply this.

Those businesses that recognize you as an individual stand out from the crowd. They know that the most successful way to deal with you as an individual is to appoint an individual on their side to be guardian of their relationship with you. Furthermore, and this is the truly distinctive aspect, in that single individual they invest finite control over all their communications with you. He or she can make the miracles happen.

Old-fashioned salespeople the world over will greet this comment with much ribald laughter and 'I told you so's'. Well, they should quieten down. They may have been right, but it is not possible that the businesses for which they worked, which employed and rewarded them the way they did, could possibly have vested this power in them. For, to be truly effective, the controller of communications must also be the controller of the relationship generally. Few business practices of the last 30 years would permit this to happen, because their structure, employee standards and the resulting regulations and safeguards precluded it.

Just as manufacturing went into mass production to achieve greater efficiency and reduced costs, so Customer service went into mass communications and mass handling methods for the same reasons. All the trends are now completely in reverse; the methods are now to do with individualization, not only in terms of the product or service, but also in terms of the relationship and recognition that is developed with the Customer.

TCM requires that communications are all ordered and enacted (or triggered) by the guardian of the relationship, since only this person knows at any given moment what the precise status quo is with any individual Customer. Thus, the Customer perceives that the right hand knows all the time what the left is doing. The Customer is never passed on to a different unknown or un-named individual; he or she never leaves the caring hands of the guardian. Never!

For those involved in mass mailings to Customers, however personalized those might be, this does not rule out anything that you are doing. It does make two important differences. First, large bulk mailings to Customers must become a thing of the past. No miracles there. The wherewithal for those mailings is now placed at the disposal of the guardians. They, in turn, feed them in to the Customer communications programme at the optimum time. Second, the communications must be seen to emanate from the guardian, not from some central point.

Many who have discovered the quite exceptional cost effectiveness of direct marketing programmes to their existing Customers may worry that the cost will increase as bulk mailing postal savings and other savings disappear. However, they can be reassured that the benefits from improved timing generally far outweigh any increased costs. After all, no one can be in a better position to know when the timing is right than the guardian. Timing is a great provider of miracles.

For those who have a logical product/service line extension there is another valuable advantage. By logical product/service line extension, I mean a range of products for which it would be possible to build a logical and progressive path of relationship building. In many cases, such ideas are not even conceivable at the moment, but they become possible with the added closeness and intimacy of the relationships that result from TCM. Financial services are ideal for this approach; so are any kind of products where the taste and style of the Customer are an issue; or even those where such apparently unlikely activities may seem foreign to relationship building, such as in professional fundraising. The ultimate product there is your last will and testament! Incidentally, my own experience in charity fundraising suggests that legacy income will increase beyond all bounds when the kinds of techniques we have discussed here are in operation.

A simple idea solves a complex problem

There are some ideas now in use that can be improved upon as you realize how profoundly the simple phrase 'it's all about Customers' could affect businesses. Let's take a typical arrangement at the moment. Suppose you're a company with four brands or product groups. Often, each group will have the freedom to choose its own ad agency; similarly, each of those same groups will appoint, or less formally, buy regularly from, its own choice of secondary specialist agency, backed up or supported by a host of PR, direct marketing, sales promotion, research and design specialists.

In organizational terms, Clients seem to have developed the people and the systems to deal with this, and, in terms of the brand or product group issues, it often works well. However, as we move into the 'brand behind the brand', and the need becomes greater for a consistent corporate voice, so such processes will break down or under-perform. It makes no sense to have a corporate message diffused, distorted or interpreted in countless different ways. It confuses the market and works badly for the company.

Shouting at the market in 10, 15 or 20 different voices represents one more dimension in the build-up to the communications traffic jam. There is a simple answer.

I have always taken the view that there are only three kinds of Customer: the existing Customer, the prospective Customer, and the lapsed or past Customer. It is generally accepted and agreed that, in terms of effectiveness from the marketing unit of currency, the highest return will come from existing Customers (typically, a performance difference of some 500–1,500 per cent), and the lowest return from prospects. However, the second-highest return comes from the group that so many people seem to overlook, or write off – the lapsed or past Customer.

Examining this, I have concluded that if – and only if – you are able to work with an integrated agency, the best way to divide the workload is to appoint the agency – across the product groups or brands – and make it 'guardian of the relationship'.

Vertical or horizontal slicing?

In Figure 7.1 'Vertical or horizontal slicing?', you can see on the vertical axis a corporate range of products and brands. The manager of each of these can fire off advertising communications or activities at will. This method of slicing the market makes good sense to the company and little or none to the Customer. It is essentially a product-driven process favoured by product managers in product-driven businesses. I call it vertical slicing.

Horizontal slicing is my preferred method. The marketplace is divided up according to the nature of the current relationship with each individual consumer or each individual organization. This will nearly always be the first segment of any segmentation hierarchy or matrix. This is a Customer-driven process, which will be the choice of Customer-driven businesses.

It is clearly pointless to try to decide the style, tone or content of any communication that respects relationships if you don't know what kind of relationship it is. Similarly, to keep those tones and values, dividing the remit of agencies along horizontal lines brings consistency. It also enables you to seek a choice of requisite agency skills to reflect the objectives you have for each agency group. They are themselves aligned to Customer groups in which the relationships are at the same stage – prospecting and acquisition, growth and loyalty building, or rescue and restoration.

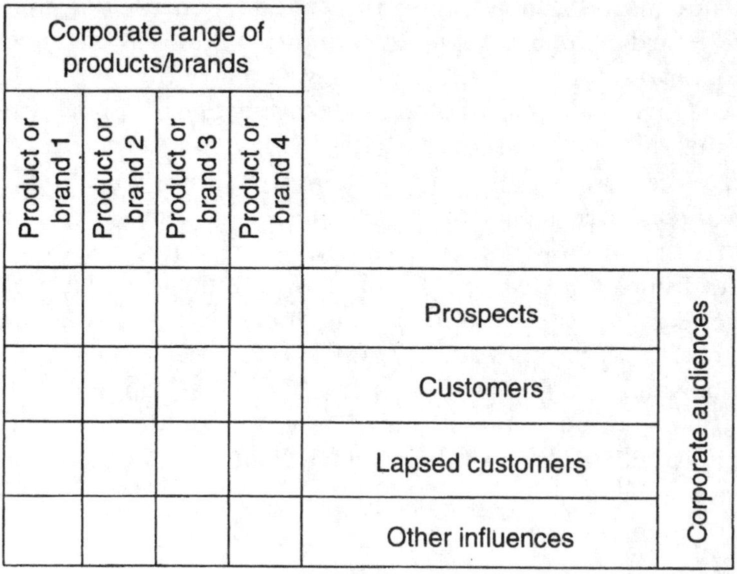

Corporate range of products/brands					
Product or brand 1	Product or brand 2	Product or brand 3	Product or brand 4		
				Prospects	Corporate audiences
				Customers	
				Lapsed customers	
				Other influences	

Figure 7.1 Vertical or horizontal slicing?

Casting your mind back to the thoughts expressed concerning the communications traffic jam, you can well understand that, if messages are confused before they leave, and are confused again as they leave the business, the result is going to be mayhem from the Customer's point of view. So, rather than having your communications disturbed and distorted, you need to find ways to improve their integrity.

There is no doubt that integration or fusion of the advertising, sales and Customer service messages is one very positive step forward. One of my Clients is a large company in the process of implementing ISMS country by country throughout Europe. There are many serious issues that arise in such large organizations, not least some structural awkwardness. For example, in the case of my Client, the Customer service team currently is to be found as part of their logistics team.

It must be realized that integrated communications, as a fundamental factor in the overall process of total communications management, are prerequisite to the concept of relationship marketing. However, the most common stumbling block is that the long-term objectives of relationship marketing, like so many quality issues, require agreement, acceptance and commitment at the very highest level. At the moment, the blossoming importance of relationship marketing and ISMS is rarely understood, let alone recognized, among board members. However committed they may be personally, marketing directors can therefore have great difficulty in carrying their colleagues along with them. Often, only one, or possibly two on the board will truly appreciate what is at stake. It is no surprise therefore that the lead is being taken by those companies who already have either a marketer at the top, or a healthily pro-marketing environment on the board. Good vision is certainly a useful lubricant to the right decisions here. Miracles come most readily when an organization gives its fullest commitment to relationship marketing and it is, therefore, no different from any quality initiative.

In the coming years, the influences that we have already discussed will push two options to the front. There is no doubt that the first of these is actually a compromise, which will enable a workable face-lift to be carried out.

Option 1: More people

In order to deliver the new relationship style of Customer service – and, therefore, the intensity of staffing required to provide the optimum server/Customer ratio – marketers will have to restructure their front line (the array they display to their Customers). Supervision and monitoring of this extended broadside exposure of their front line will be handled on a database; Customer communications of whatever type will be focused via, or in support of, the individual Customer servicer or Customer services team, but always through (or acknowledged by) a database.

This will lead to an increase in teams, structured in many ways in a style familiar to marketers, similar to that found inside advertising agencies – a triangular-shaped team with three or four levels. However, I described this as cosmetic and a compromise. And it is so. For on a short-term basis it will enable the Customer to feel as if he or she is getting more service. What is actually happening is that the Customer is getting more attention. This is not in itself a problem, but it is still far short of what is needed for a truly effective relationship to develop. Such service teams are usually long on bonhomie and rhetoric but short on the authority and decision-making capability that is needed.

So why is this a compromise? Why is it less likely to succeed? Consider this scenario. In comes a wealth of new communications technology. This is irresistible to people involved in Customer service. And understandably, after all, much of the time the pressure to accept or adopt new-tech communications methods or media comes from the markets or Customers they serve.

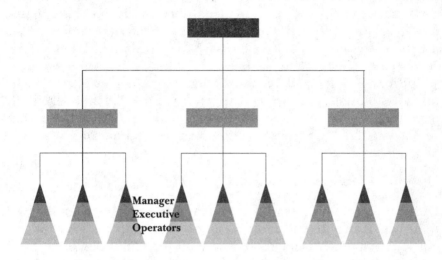

Figure 7.2 The modified hierarchy – the micro-hierarchy within a hierarchy

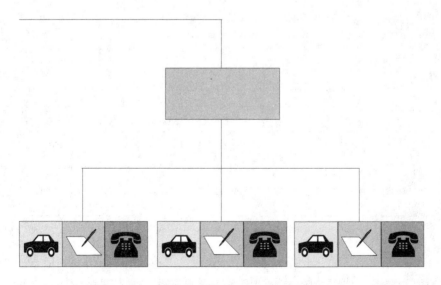

Figure 7.3 A common division of labour within a Customer service micro-hierarchy

Next, let's fuel this with the certain knowledge that the easiest way to show a quick, or cosmetic, increase in Customer care or service is to communicate more, stay in touch, keep the Customer informed. This means, of course, that in order to make the necessary impression on Customers, more people in more departments will want to communicate more ways through more media. And if you're dealing with an organization, more people will receive these communications across correspondingly more departments. Think how much this will be a recipe for confusion and irritation. Simply stir in the media and technology explosions that we see happening in parallel and bake well. Soon you'll have a perfect disaster in the making. All covered in that confection of the future – the communications traffic jam!

Option 2: More sense

Option 1 is only for those who want an interim measure to Option 2 or those who are content with the cosmetic improvement. It is a bit of a quick fix! Option 2 is for those who want the real thing; but it does mean that you must seek out suppliers who offer you integrated marketing services. And then appoint them as guardians as one of the three basic relationships. At the very simplest, there are only three categories of Customer – those you have, those you don't have yet, and those you did have, but lost. In your forward external marketing thrust, you are basically cultivating three corresponding categories of relationship as illustrated in Table 7.1.

Table 7.1 Relationship styles and objectives

CATEGORY	STYLE	OBJECTIVE
Prospects	Warming	Acquisition
Customers	Satisfying	Growth
Lapsed and past Customers	Restoring	Reconciliation

To maintain the integrity of corporate voices, the responsibility for communications should be divided within these relationship objectives. Thus, one agency might be appointed guardian of existing

Customers; this agency will have demonstrated its ability to create powerful advertising and sales messages that respect the Customers, understand their needs, and speak with one corporate voice. As with the other two categories, this cuts across all brands, products, or services. Only where there is no 'cross-talk' or cross-selling opportunity with brands would division of guardianship by brand be recommended.

This clearly suggests that the formal division between the disciplines (advertising, sales promotion, direct marketing, PR, and so on), running as they do in tightly defined alleys, must dissolve, or at lease assume far less priority. The overall basket of media, and the uses to which those media are put, will fall along with the whole gamut of Customer service activities into a Total Communications Management environment. There, with the marketing database as its core resource, the individual relationship with the Customer will take its rightful place as the driving force. This should provide a perfect culture for optimum Customer service levels and standards. In those companies where marketing and sales remain uneasy bed partners, such new thinking will be difficult to accept since they must clearly come together as one redefined effort.

So, the new picture will include fused sales, marketing and service teams also dividing their efforts into the three steps of acquisition, growth and reconciliation, each representing the full basket of products and services to Customers – even if one is selected at any given time for tactical, timing or other reasons.

One of the points raised by reorganizing this way is what happens to the brand and, as I mentioned earlier, the increasingly significant 'brand behind the brand'? I accept that this difficulty, creating cohesion and harmony between the work of different agencies and other suppliers still exists. However, my belief is that any lack of cohesion in brand delivery by your agencies is a lot less discernible to Customers if it takes place at the time of natural shifts in the relationship stage, than if it happens constantly during the relationship while the Customer is bombarded by communications from various product streams.

In come the New Wave

The problems and opportunities with communication of the brand exist whether you use the old methods or the new. What will change a great deal, however, is the marketing business itself, and how advertisers and marketers relate to it and the demands they make of it. There will surely be a New Wave Client needing a New Wave agency.

The heyday of many of the distinct or discrete marketing disciplines may soon be over. Will we see the death of direct marketing, the demise of PR, or the end of sales promotion? I don't think so! There will, of course, be many special cases, or smaller Clients who will continue to use the resources of marketing services as we know them now. But, in some years' time, the serious spenders will have gone back to the 1950s and once again appointed their agencies to do it all. These agencies are being born right now. They are the result of new ideas, new thinking, new Customer needs and desires, new technology and a new environment.

What of the product manager?

I suspect that the days of the function of product manager as we know it are numbered. The days of the market or 'Customer group' manager are beginning to be realized. For the product manager usually has a corporate orientation to the market, the other has a market orientation to the Customer. This is the stuff of New Wave Clients. With a bank of product managers, Customer communications lack flow, cohesion and integrity for the Customer. For each product manager has his or her own priorities – product priorities. With a bank of market or Customer managers, each has his or her own priorities too – but they are always Customer priorities.

So let's close this chapter with the story of a mail order business for whom I adapted the same concept as the bank entry system, but for their telemarketing team. First, we channelled Customer groups around operator teams, to allow people to get to know each other. Next, we graded the Customers and set service standards for the grades. Then we sat back and watched these people – predominantly women – get to know each other. Abundant miracles!

Indeed, it went so well that we introduced a phase two, encouraging the telemarketers to make outbound 'social' calls to the higher-priority Customers. As I explained at the beginning of this book, some of my best stories have to stay anonymous. So I can't say more – other than that sales have gone through the roof! I mean through the roof! This was one of my best schemes. Don't ask my Client. Ask her Customers who will tell you that they have never experienced anything like it in their lives.

However, we must watch the dangers as technology provides more and more ways for us to communicate with each other. It will mean, if we do not take these communications seriously, that 'junk' communications could proliferate – 'spamming' could come to many of them. This will force the consumer or Customer to build defence mechanisms, and rightly so.

With portable faxes, cellphones, phones in planes and almost everywhere else, global universal telephone numbers, e-mail, voice mail, and computer contact from almost anywhere, in any hotel – or, indeed from any phone socket – readily available for years, we are potentially on the verge of a traffic jam for the Customer. The very best way to show that you wish to distance yourself from that whole game is to bring integrity to your Customer relationships. That means letting the Customer decide how they would prefer to hear from you, using Total Communications Management, bringing your communications into real time and making them as relevant as possible to the individual who is receiving them. In other words, it's all about Customers!

Let's take a run through the major topics of this chapter – as harmless as they might seem at the moment, they will prove to be among the most pivotal for your business in the future.

● We are in danger of witnessing (or becoming involved in) a communications traffic jam of global proportions. This will be caused by an increasing number of people wishing to communicate with the Customer and the rapidly increasing communications media and opportunities they will have at their disposal. This jam will alienate Customers and prospects alike.
● Customer service levels should not decrease as the quantity of Customers increases. Indeed, the reverse should be true.
● Total Communications Management (TCM) provides an effective method of organizing and controlling *all* the elements of the Client relationship and thereby adding significant timing benefits to repeat or cross-selling activities.
● TCM delivers improvements to marketing effectiveness by maximizing all the elements of the Client relationship and thereby adding significant timing benefits to repeat or cross-selling activities.
● To enable ISMS and relationship marketing – and for apportioning work to agencies – it is better to switch to horizontal slicing of the audience as opposed to vertical slicing.

- Marketing work will become increasingly specialized in the three areas that recognize the three types of Customer: prospective, existing and lapsed.
- Customer service teams face two options: the first is to increase manpower to provide a better Customer/servicer ratio. However, this is usually only capable of cosmetic, short-term gains. The second option is to rationalize the sales and marketing forces in the same way as the new agencies. This method provides powerful, sensitive marketing with integrity of corporate and brand voice.
- Companies with a marketer at the top, or in which a pro-marketing environment exists at board level, will make these changes fastest and will steal a valuable lead on their opposition.
- Few companies appreciate how to distinguish between high-potential and low-potential Customers in respect of loyalty and equally few understand how this can be used in the acquisition of new business.
- The function of product manager could soon become quite rare. They will be replaced by market managers whose priorities are Customer priorities.

8

Selling has passed its sell-by date

A short but telling article appeared in the British *Sunday Times* a few years ago. It commented as follows:

> Criticism of sales methods employed by photocopier distributors has prompted Southern Business Group to introduce a code of conduct for its salesforce. Central to the code will be a 14-day 'cooling-off' period similar to that in the life insurance sector allowing Customers the chance to consider the implications of any service or leasing agreement. It is a reform other distributors would do well to follow.

Fantastic! This simply says, 'We're going to go on cheating and lying. But if you're smart enough to spot that we ripped you off within 14 days, we'll work something out. If you spot it after 14 days you can go to hell just like you did before!'

For the life of me, I could not work out why the *Sunday Times*, which had previously led a witchhunt against this type of malpractice, was not asking the obvious question. For me, the obvious question was, 'Why don't you fire the cheating, lying no-goods who are bringing the company into disrepute and running round conning Customers simply so they can pocket the commission?'

This chapter covers ground that may be difficult for many to accept. Not because its thesis is complex or hard to absorb, but because of the challenge it makes and the investment it requires. It may seem to exacerbate what certain people choose to see as a prejudice against selling and sales ideas. It is of course difficult to point out weaknesses, suggest modifications or demonstrate new methods without some implicit criticism of the past or even of the status quo. Traditional salespeople could look at my career in marketing and claim that the grudge has tumbled out of my head and on to the page. I feel that if I at least make my personal position clear then those who feel they have spotted prejudice will at least have the measure of it.

I have always considered that I hold the strategic views of a marketer and the tactical skills of a salesperson. In relation to the art of selling, I have, when appropriate (and that was often), energetically and enthusiastically worked to bring a high level of professionalism to this. In my view, you can only be a professional salesperson when you have an understanding of both the value and process of marketing and of the business in general. Equally, the business can only fully appreciate the salesperson when it understands that it is the salesperson, generally, who achieves the successful results that are the testimony to the organization's overall ability. When it's working well, it's truly teamwork. Despite this, which I feel is a rather balanced disposition, it has never been difficult for me to accept that selling is a function of marketing.

What has selling been all about?

Let's not beat about the bush. Let's leap in with both feet and alienate a whole group of people! Here goes...

For decades, selling has *not* been about the Customer. Selling has been about the product or service. This is actually neither new nor prejudiced thinking. The eminent Professor Kotler's late 1970s paper 'From Sales Obsession to Marketing Effectiveness' suggests that 'selling focuses on the needs of the seller. It is preoccupied with the seller's need to convert his product to cash.'

Imagine that I own a factory. It makes widgets. My factory makes widgets five days a week. By Friday, the warehouse is full, and I have nowhere to put next week's widgets. I'd better get a salesforce.

'OK, salespeople, get out there and sell these widgets. The more you sell, the more you earn.' They clear the warehouse. But the factory goes on manufacturing and the staff and the overheads need paying, and the suppliers too. Better get the salesforce back, the warehouse is full again and I need to collect the money they've raised from the first lot. In comes the salesforce. It leaves the money and clears the warehouse again! This cycle goes on all very nicely for a few weeks, except soon the salesforce seems to be having some trouble clearing the whole warehouse.

'We're selling as many widgets as we can, but it's getting harder to find new Customers and we need something extra to tempt people to buy more.'

'OK, salesforce, give them a discount.' The warehouse is empty again, but only for a day or so; soon, the relentless production at the factory has filled it up again. 'Get back here salespeople, my warehouse is full again.'

'But it's only Thursday – and we've still got problems getting rid of last week's production.'

'Give 'em a BOGOF.'

'What's that?'

'Buy One, Get One Free! Now BOGOF out of here and get going. And don't forget to leave the money!'

As the salesforce clears the warehouse yet again, their eyes boggle. It is bursting at the seams and the next week's production is filling up the shelves at one end as they're clearing the other. What can they do next to Customers and prospects to make them buy more?

Selling had to manipulate to succeed

I have taken you through the Toytown example above to illustrate my point. You can see from this that Kotler is right. Selling is, or has certainly become, a manipulative and exploitative process. It is obsessed with quantity. It sets its objectives by quantity. It rewards by quantity. It is an aggressive, offensive action.

I remind you, this is not a criticism. It is a statement of fact. The transition to this posture took place over the mid-1950s and early to mid-1960s. It was the beginning of the end for Customer care as a way of life and, to a great extent, for the kind of salesperson who put the relationship they created with the Customer first and foremost, and the selling second.

Whether Professor Kotler had an academic crystal-ball mentality, or whether the USA got there first we can speculate. Certainly, to many nations, American methods became the role model of the quantity selling age. Or were they just a little more extreme than others?

Now the time has come for salespeople to look at the new challenge, to examine the ways of the past 30 years and to decide how they can maintain the quantity but develop methods that do not leave devastation and a trail of bodies behind them. This is not as hard as it seems. Improved communications, databases, software and all manner of aids are becoming available to assist. But the old-fashioned sales director or vice-president, that John Wayne-like charismatic super-hero who led his salesforce like some cavalier hit squad, is well on his way out. These days, he looks like something from an old black and white 'B' movie!

I recently wrote a book about sales management in the new culture. In fact, this book was commissioned for internal use by a financial services Client company. It was to help them inculcate their new relationship marketing culture as they implemented ISMS and set about becoming a Customer-driven business. In it, I wrote the following: 'The future is different. It's better...but harder....

> The fact is that teams can be run democratically or autocratically. The culture by which your sales team was run for many years was autocratic. And, to be fair, so were almost all the others. Businesses used to be run like armies. The centre of control and command was at the top. The managing director effectively dictated the direction of the business and charged his fellow directors with implementing his plan. The MD's job was to get the maximum return for the shareholders by screwing as much out of Customers as they could. The directors interpreted the bosses' plan and handed it down to their managers, who worked out the detail and created the implementation plans. They then passed these plans on to the lower levels of management, who figured out what to do and issued instructions to the staff. The staff then did as they were told or got fired.
>
> In those days, Customers got what they were given, which was what the company had decided to sell or offer. Or, as came to be the case with financial services for many years, the Customer was cajoled – even tricked in the worst cases – into buying anything that made a fast buck for the sales team and seemed to make a good sale for the business. Everyone was chasing new business. What happened to the Customer after the sale only mattered if he or she had more money to spend. It's a sorry tale, and no wonder really that regulation was to be the end result. Frankly, it is a miracle that it is still self-regulation. The whole thing was driven by greed. Of course, it couldn't last. Customers rebelled. No Customers, it became clear, meant no return for shareholders. MDs and CEOs globally went into a quick huddle in their changing room and came out 'new men' and 'new women'.
>
> So now, quite rightly, we are seeing the pendulum swing the other way. Indeed, I am proud to be a vocal crusader and campaigner in the cause of bringing the old ways to an end. More, I am totally committed

to helping businesses turn round, become Customer-facing, and learn how to deliver the new (or should that be old?) standards and practices.

The reason for this history lesson is to explain, to some extent, why salespeople must spend so much time and concentrate so much effort in coming to terms with so many new practices and an almost totally new culture. Senior management is now looking for enterprise and initiative from its stars. In the days of the old culture, the one who did as he or she was told the best, or the most, became the star. The new culture appreciates that you and your team are out there with the Customer. You see, hear and feel their needs. It is in assisting you to meet those needs that your management can best achieve the aims of the business.

In simple terms, the energies and dynamics of many businesses have turned, or are turning, completely about-face. So, as well as learning to take on these new cultures, to restructure, to deliver improved service, to re-engineer processes to be faster, lower cost and more accurate, and to put back a quality ethos into sales and marketing, the whole life assurance business has been handed a double whammy of the worst kind. An already flat market has had to cope with enormous self-regulation and disclosure too.

Now you may have been a sales manager for some years and it would be very easy for you to sit back and say, 'I'm OK. I've been a manager quite a while. I know how to do it. I don't need this book.' Take that risk at your peril. For in the 'new' Customer-focused ethos, the task and role of the sales manager has changed radically. You are no longer an officer on HMS Command and Control. It's no longer about flogging stuff as hard as you can and standing behind your lads with a whip, keeping them at it, hyping them up. Now the company has explicit objectives to deliver a quality-based service-oriented method of gaining sales, which is arrived at by making the vehicle for sales achievement a strong, caring and satisfying relationship. It's a whole new way of getting business. Today's sales manager is predominantly a coach, a counsellor and trainer. There's an emotional and psychological content to your work which just wasn't there before.

This is all going to have an enormous effect on the skills that are required by salespeople. In a sense, they have to come to terms with the difference between the power to profit versus the power to please. This, particularly, will put the greatest pressure on the sales managers as they get to grips with their new role.

Definite miracles to be found in this area.

Preparing for change

The practice of selling has much change to make; however, in writing this section, I am aware that it needs to be sensitively handled. There is a danger that many groups of salespeople might be alienated because they interpret the comments I am about to make as, at best, critical and, at worst, offensive. This would be completely counterproductive. Sales, marketing and service should be totally harmonious processes. However, many changes are already taking place that dictate a change in selling style. By implication, the proposal of new methods seems to criticize the old ones; in this case, that is true. The old ways were appropriate for their time. Now they are not. This point may become clearer when you consider the Three Generations of Selling.

At first glance, to a salesperson who matured during the 1970s and 1980s especially, this view of the future might seem a little lacking in aggression. Again, that's true. The sales style that goes with a Customer-driven business is softer. It is assertive rather than aggressive; anxious to serve the company's own best interests through serving their Customer.

Although I describe the selling style as softer, the new selling methods are harder to achieve. They require long-term commitment from the top and selfless dedication to the Customer from all the individuals concerned. To be clear, I am not suggesting that all salespeople and organizations will change to these new methods. I expect to see plenty of all three generations around in the future. Some organizations will prefer to stay with the methods they know – the familiar ways that have served them well. Others will move ahead with time, learning the newer, more caring processes and appreciating the stability and value this will add to their company, their career and their life. Customers definitely prefer the newer methods and this may indeed provide the greatest impetus for change.

The three generations of selling

As you look back over the past decades, it becomes clear that the business of selling did not escape the helter-skelter down the quantity route. In fact, during the eras of mass production and mass marketing, it would be fair to say that selling was in the front line. As the quantity target pressures built up, it was the refinement of sales techniques and promotion – the ability to manipulate markets and exploit sales opportunities to a greater degree – that carried both the greatest work-load and the greatest responsibility. It was not uncommon in many companies to see the marketing department reduced, from its strategic and principled role, to a mere inventor of constant merchandising, promotional and incentive programmes. It is no wonder that the infamous idea of marginal costing sprang to popularity in these times.

These were the days when the concept that 'the Customer is king' was a means to an end; the end was the heavily disguised truth that the product was actually king.

The first generation of selling

As we moved through the 1990s, any lingering doubt that we lived in a 'benefits' society faded. We bought things for what they did for our lifestyle. In the 1960s and early 1970s we were deeply embedded in a 'features' society. The ads for cars carried checklists inviting you to compare feature for feature. We switched from black and white TV to the newly featured colour. In the post-war years across the world, we moved from scarce availability to overloaded markets groaning with products that needed to be pumped down the distribution channel with great effort and energy. Eventually, many markets moved into glut. The consumer revelled as prices dropped, and gradually we saw families with two cars, a TV in several rooms and a dishwasher. It could be well argued that what I describe as the first generation of selling was not actually the first at all. It developed during the age of glut; it was a natural evolution from the heavy-advertising, heavy-selling time. I call it the first generation because it was the pre-decessor of the following generations.

In searching for a word to describe the style of selling of this era, the word 'muscular' comes to mind and seems to fit admirably. To be sold to was almost to be press-ganged. Lessons in selling were given by guru figures, who presented themselves to hundreds of avaricious life assurance salesmen, who worshipped them as if they were indeed some new God; they were Masters of their Universe; Kings of the silver tongue and the smooth psychology that left a Customer with no more 'No's'. So the only result was 'Yes'. Conquest. The commission register would ring up another sale.

The language of this generation was aggressive and, in its literal sense, offensive. Those salespeople 'attacked' a market. Their whole *modus operandi* was military. Of course, it led to some jolly good annual sales conferences. Great praise was heaped upon the salesperson who browbeat the most Customers into taking the most goods. But nobody stopped to think how the Customer felt about all this. Why bother? The sale was everything. The commission cheque mere confirmation that winning the great sales race was what life was all about.

It was all very simple in the days of the first generation. You sold a product and people bought its production; or, if you were a consumer, its features. We bought lawnmowers because they cut lawns; pop-up toasters because they popped up; copiers because they copied; typewriters because they typed. Gradually, through the latter part of the 1970s and into the 1980s, a new generation was born.

The second generation of selling

This was the time when selling started to deal with the notion of added value. Those who had learned that competitive discounting led to a war of attrition turned their attention to increasing Customer satisfaction and looking beyond the product.

Five-year warranty and extended service packages were invented. Computers came with software and games. Televisions (and just about every other domestic appliance possible!) came with infrared remote control. 'Have a nice day' came to Europe. Those who bought copiers because they copied bought them now because they copied faster, as well as collating, printing front and back, on plain paper, and came with a service contract. Those who bought typewriters because they typed bought something entirely new. It was called a word processor. It was absolutely useless. Unless, of course, you bought the added-value package that gave you the equipment plus a training programme. And as a result, now, one word processor operator could do the work of two or three typists. But only with the training.

Suddenly the added-value age was upon us. It sold the product, but also sold the skills that helped the Customer get the best out of it. Suddenly, what Customers were buying was no longer the product. It was increased productivity.

I call the selling style for this generation 'cupped hands'. For many consumers, added value brought the promise of better service. However, in this generation it was a fairly cosmetic operation. It culminated in the seed corn of the Age of the Customer. Hotels started to put photographs of their management in their lobby; name badges became the order of the day; banks encouraged their tellers to smile; the shopping mall was discovered in Europe. The Customer mistook this patronizing lip service for the real thing and was momentarily content. Hip organizations trained their telephone operators to answer, 'Good Morning. Thank you for calling the Hayling Island Post House. Sharon speaking. How may I help you?' Telephone companies announced record profits! The Customer service campaign – the non-thinking person's answer to 'In Search of Excellence' – was under way. Meanwhile, the thinking man and woman were at work looking into the way genuine change needed to happen beneath the veneer. And they found a miracle waiting to happen. As so often seems to be the case, it had a problem attached! However, without solving the problem, the next generation could not happen.

Preparing for the new age of selling

I remember sitting with a sales manager of a Client company. He had been with the business for nearly 30 years. For the vast majority of that time he had been on the sales side of the business and for some years he had led the sales team at one of the top-selling branches in the business. I was there to give a talk to his team and support staff about 'the new way' – the style and culture shift the company was making to bring its practices into line with the Customer philosophy set out in its mission statement. As he summed up at the end, he turned to me and, in front of his team, said, 'I agree with every single word that's been said here today. And…' he turned back to face his assembled team, 'that's why I'm going to need help from all of you. I know the old way like the back of my hand. I've been the best or second- or third-best in this company every year for damn near two decades. As I've been doing the old stuff the longest, I reckon these new ideas will take a while to become second nature to me. So I need your help to make sure that I make them happen. And you need mine. So we're in it together. Just like normal!'

Our friend had raised a moot point. He had realized that, as a sales manager, he had the dilemma of being simultaneously the person who had to build conviction in, commitment to, and skills in, the new culture and style of selling while also being the team member who was most entrenched in the old ways. The last 20 years of his working life had constantly reinforced and confirmed that he was succeeding by getting it right and by being good at selling. Now, quite suddenly, he was to become, for his team, the changemaster of something new and different. I knew what he was thinking, as we had talked earlier. His unspoken question was this: 'I know it sounds right. But will it work?' Doubt is an uneasy place from which to lead change.

From master salesperson to mentor, motivator and manager

Those who criticize the notion of top sales performers becoming sales managers seem to make a fair point. Yet, if they're right, why do so many, many companies go on promoting such people? Why do so many sales directors keep choosing them? Why do CEOs keep approving it?

The answer is because, in many cases, it works. It works because top salespeople are usually bright and intelligent, and 'people' people. Such men and women like new challenges and can learn. But, most importantly, they can sell themselves and their ideas. This is one of the greatest characteristics of good leadership.

However, the good and effective sales managers must quickly catch hold of the value of strong and powerful leadership, and understand what, in today's management culture, 'strong and powerful leadership' means. Tomorrow's manager will have to support his or her team in the 'new ways', and lead by example.

Leadership in a Customer-driven business is about recognizing how much of the management task is in the mentor and motivator roles. And it's about realizing how very, very little lies in telling people what to do. Instead of telling people what to do, leaders must help them to know what to do. They must help them to acknowledge and understand their own successes and failures, and help them to find their true potential. Leaders support, counsel, encourage, demonstrate and coach.

Not many of the old-fashioned sales leaders would recognize this kind of language. Look at the last few words of the last paragraph again: 'support, counsel, encourage, demonstrate and coach'. It's rather different from the ways of the past. And unfortunately, as I have pointed out earlier, many of the people – and I don't just refer to sales managers here, but all senior people – who have to make the decision for this change, and lead it through, are those self-same individuals who climbed the ladder using their old skills! Catch 22! Those who can make it happen are leading us into...

The third generation of selling

We're heading into the Age of Individualization and back to relationship values. But beware, for in both the consumer and business markets, the Customer's expectation has changed, and so, to a degree, has what they're out there buying.

Take the business market. In previous generations we saw the type-writer become the word processor; and we saw how the skills that went with it gave it the added value of increased productivity for the Customer. Here, in the third generation, the seller and the buyer join together to decide what the buyer needs and how best it can be supplied. Thus, the company that sold the word processor would now sit down with its Customer to decide together how the seller's skills can best be made to work together to fill the buyer's needs for the future.

The word processor manufacturer might find out that his Customer, a publisher, is looking to computerize his typesetting so that it can be written as raw journalistic input, be checked and edited by a third party, then be moved down the line to typesetting and page make-up, and on again to print. The publisher is looking to buy the seller's know-how – the equipment or hardware becomes a secondary part of the whole process.

Table 8.1 The three generations of selling

PHASE	TECHNIQUE	WHAT YOU SELL	WHAT THEY BUY
FIRST GENERATION	Selling	The product	Production
SECOND GENERATION	Added-value selling	The product with skills	Productivity
THIRD GENERATION	Multi-discipline marketing	Know-how (opportunity)	Ideas (opportunity)

Is what you are selling what people want to buy?

For more and more markets, the product is becoming a know-how product. Oddly, since know-how is being sold and ideas, therefore, are being bought, it seems to me that, finally, selling's evolutionary process has arrived at a conclusion where, possibly in many markets, the two have become the same for the very first time. Both represent opportunity. That is what is being sold and that is what is being bought.

This concept of know-how as a product is fast gaining recognition in many business markets and in certain consumer markets, such as financial services. It has an irrefutable logic. Which makes more sense to you? Consider the choices:

- the machine itself – a first-generation product;
- the machine tailored to your specification or with the added value of skill opportunities to get the best out of it;
- or the machine designed to do a better job for you tomorrow because it is the result of a team effort involving the brains at the buying company and the brains at the manufacturer?

This is the first part of the Age of Individualization in which the third generation of selling excels. Yet individualization promises more – it promises recognition, and a level of personal service that is both enticing and captivating. It promises to make it all about Customers.

As we reviewed the shift in selling style, we saw the following.

- Selling has not been a Customer-driven process for decades. It has been a production-driven process.
- Selling has required that the market be manipulated and exploited to achieve its aims.
- Selling has sadly become a process that is over-influenced by the quantity obsession and shorter-term objectives have thus won out over longer-term objectives; the sale has taken precedence over the Customer relationship. In effect, this means that the second sale has lost out to the first!
- Salespeople, especially those who lead sales teams, have to learn a whole host of new leadership and management skills.
- Selling is entering a time of a softer style than has been used for 30 years or more.
- The Three Generations of Selling track the styles through time and identify know-how as a major new 'product' for the future.

9

The relationship to structure

When considering the question of organizational restructuring, a central issue will be in the provision of a structure that will support ISMS – integrated sales, marketing and service. The three must integrate. We've tried co-operation – it ends in bloodshed at worst, and frustration and exasperation at best.

I expect many companies, in practice, actually cease to draw a distinction between the three functions over the years. There is so little merit in so many cases. It can already be argued that all marketing, in one guise or another, is selling; it is only a matter of time before the reverse should become true and all selling will become marketing. At that point, distinction loses reason.

Restructuring to become a Customer-driven business should not be a marketing department decision. It is a board decision. Without the complete buy-in of all, and without the direct, visible and total support of the CEO, it will fail. Where I have witnessed the process kept as a marketing decision and a marketing process, it tends to be viewed by others as some kind of mental aberration by marketing, or a power play to take over the world! Oddly, in one or two cases, the biggest resistance comes from sales!

A new balance and therefore a new balance of power

At the moment, convention suggests that a business has assets – its buildings, machinery, plant, people and expertise. With manufacturing businesses the valuation of assets is quite traditional; with service businesses this matter is more complicated, since its people are often a more important factor. However, in tomorrow's businesses we see two other assets that become significant. The problem for accountants is that these two assets are both intangible.

The first asset is know-how and the second is Customer relationships. In the latter area, some pioneering work is being done, and I expect to see accounting conventions come to terms with this new thinking. More importantly, we need to appreciate that, as we move from transactions to relationships, in the fundamental shift of a Customer-driven business, so we will no longer see individual sales transactions as the units of currency. Focus is shifted on to the building of relationships. Customer relationships are more stable, more predictable, more reliable, but still, at this time, less quantifiable to accountants. Over time, as the power and effectiveness and, therefore, the value of these relationships starts to outshine the traditional methods, so this will create a shift in balance of the perceived assets and their value to the company.

For many, a new view will develop, which is that the market is a greater asset than the business. In other words, instead of building a business and constantly looking for markets to satisfy it, the balance changes to the view that says we have the market – that is, the power – and we must look for manufacturing or service opportunities to satisfy it. So these are the two extremes of view; where your company positions itself is what matters. For the future, however, we can be sure of a substantial swing towards those which place quite significant value on the markets. A point which, incidentally, juxtaposes quite favourably with the 1980s trends of looking anew at the asset value of brands. Indeed, if you have observed how investment decisions have been magnified since the notion that brands have quantifiable asset values, you can imagine how the same concept applies to Customer relationships.

Will the board understand the decision it will be asked to make?

The extent of restructuring, and the making of the decision by the board, presents, I believe, two substantial hurdles. The first is to gain sufficient understanding of the new concepts through to those representing (and usually protective of) their own disciplines and territories. The impact on them is quite extensive if it is to be a corporate restructure. For the autonomous business units that result, operating as if they are, in effect, small businesses-within-businesses will integrate sales, marketing and service and, in the process, devolve them down to the front. We are dealing with a potentially highly charged political issue! Thus, those who are making the case for this change must have a full and clear understanding of all the wider business issues before they go to the board.

The Customer-driven business model can be used to provide a common-sense case – which is irrefutable – and a financial case. For the financial case, think of the model as a series of business processes and calculate the financial improvement against present practices. However, you should be warned that this can be a lengthy business, and I have twice seen businesses grappling with the development of a financial business case overtaken by competitors who were becoming Customer-driven because they thought it was right. These competitors go past at the speed of light, since they combine the commitment, zeal and passion of those doing something they believe in – unlike those who hesitate, display doubts and fears, and endlessly do their sums.

Back to the Customer yet again

What should lie behind the structural shape of a company? What is wrong with a hierarchy?

Common sense tells us that, if the majority accept, as is traditional, one common shape to solve all problems, then that shape must have more to do with its suitability for the problem solver than it does with the problem to be solved. If the business world consists of problems that fall into four types – rivets, screws, nuts and nails – having a hammer will perform a task, but it will be much more effective in certain identifiable cases. Those who argue for the hammer, in praise of hierarchies, will suggest that the well-being of the problem solver is important, since no good at all will come of a broken hammer. Those who favour autonomous business units, while agreeing that having all four of the necessary tools requires more skills, equally accept that the end result is vastly better, since you find the right solution to the right problem.

Customer-driven marketing places the Customer first – even in this decision. For the structure of the business should facilitate its primary function. The primary function of the business is to respond to Customer needs. The optimum way to achieve this is through flexible, agile, high-energy, responsible teams. Further, to stay flexible to Customers and markets, the structures that are developed should themselves be under constant review.

What do Customers want of us? How do they use our products or services? What will they need from us next? These are the real issues for determining a corporate structure. Find these answers and the board will find its structural answers.

Elegance of form

There is one further idea that you might like to think about when looking at organizational structures. Draw them on paper, to see how they look. For me, one of the great plus points of the hierarchy was that it had elegance of form. When the elegance was there it usually worked well. When managers had distorted the hierarchy to a shape lacking elegance, it looked as clumsy as its performance proved to be.

This idea does not suggest that effective organizational structures always look good on paper or, even more ridiculously, that if it does not work on paper, it won't work in fact. It does propose that structures that look right are more likely to work right, whether they are hierarchies or not.

The death of the middle manager

It is at least a decade and a half, maybe more, since Professor Peter Druker, at the time internationally lauded Professor of Social Services and Management at the Claremont Graduate School in California, predicted with unnerving accuracy the de-massification of corporate infrastructures that is now happening all around us. Professor Druker suggested the following:

> The typical large business 20 years hence will have fewer than half the levels of management…and no more than one-third of the managers.

The prediction proved faulty only in that the change started sooner than Professor Druker suggested, and is taking business far too long to complete. De-massification is under way on a national and international scale.

If you're a middle manager, look out for your job! It could dissolve before your eyes; at least, it is in severe danger of doing so. That may not be so bad, since you may end up having much more fun, enjoying much more stimulation and getting far greater satisfaction in the Customer-facing jobs that are bound to increase. There, you'll be involved with real live Customers, and getting to grips with events and actualities that really matter. It feels great. And the most significant element is that more and more people are discovering the satisfaction, pleasure and fulfilment of attending Customers' needs and desires. It is actually what business is for. Yet there is a massive dilemma. This whole preoccupation with de-massifying companies is further confused by the de-massifying markets. Now, to achieve our objectives in business, we may have to look at fragments of fragments.

Let's examine Professor Druker's original premise and luxuriate in the benefit of hindsight. Further, let's look at the validity it holds for a Customer-driven business. My confession is one of bias. In the mid-1980s, I was correctly quoted as saying I would rather run a networked group of small agencies than one large one. The danger is that you set up an evolutionary continuum; no sooner have you unbundled the whole group than someone has the fabulous idea of creating a central resource for something. Then the overheads of all the different units are examined against the reduced costs of a bundled unit under one roof; the costs and facility of communications are reviewed and, surprise, surprise, they too would be improved in one building. What people forget is that you lose speed and flexibility.

Think Customer. What's best for the Customer? For example, in the case of an ad agency, there is nothing that a small agency can't do as well as a big agency. It's generally only big for its own sake. This is actually true of many businesses.

Look at your own business. Think Customer. Question why your business is the size it is. Search for justifications. Generally, there are plenty, but few of them are to do with the Customer.

Think Customer. Examine your processes. Your systems. Your structure. Your culture. Look at everything. Examine the real benefits of size. But when you look at each facet, evaluate it with those two words up front. Think Customer.

Examine the role of your people. How many touch Customers? How many exist for the benefit of the momentum of the business? How many come to work – and how many come to serve the Customers by serving the business? You'll find that the more people you have who are involved with Customers, the more motivated they are. In today's hi-tech, automatic, computerized, digital work society, every business has to become a people business. Otherwise the motivation goes. You can only play computer games for so long.

In a way it is this scenario that lies behind Druker's thesis. So many businesses have become glorified data-processing machines. I recall in this respect those cartoons that appeared in the 1960s. They wryly poked fun at the executive who returned from lunch only to find that he'd been replaced by a computer. The marginal inaccuracy was that, in fact, whole layers of the business were being made redundant.

If you stand back and observe businesses, you can clearly see their data processing at work. The front line gathers data like scurrying ants. Often, like ants, they gather more than their own weight! They return to base and pass the data to their managers. The managers sift and batch the data and pass it with a satisfied smile up to the next level. The next level devours the data hungrily. What is there here that can help the decision-making process? Finally, with decisions identified and the data processed and transformed into information, it arrives at the top, ready for the decision to be made. Once the information has been considered and the decision made, the whole process starts up once more, but in reverse. The first level down takes the decision and forms an implementation plan. The departmental or divisional responsibilities are handed down and the news finally reaches the front line, where our scurrying ant-like creatures dash frantically in and out of the marketplace excitedly going about their business. It is a very cumbersome, costly and time-consuming process.

So, when you analyse many a big corporation, and identify the tasks where being big or bigger is genuinely useful – in other words, it adds something for the Customer – you find they are few and far between. At least they are when you bear in mind that, in a networked group of autonomous business units, most of the benefits still exist. For example, nobody has done away with the range of experience, or the diverse skills of the workforce, or the buying power, and so on. The result of such an analysis leads to the de-massification process that Druker predicted; many companies have now found that this process leaves them in far better shape. And, importantly, the flatter structure moves the heart of the company nearer to the Customers and makes the unit far more responsive to their needs. However, I maintain, reducing the hierarchy alone is not sufficient. A hierarchy is only a mechanism to appease the fragility of mankind.

The essential accompaniments to restructuring also include a radical change in management style and culture. Leadership becomes a key issue, too. I know of a company with a multi-million pound change project on hand at the moment; I suspect that it will fail for one reason, and one reason only. The CEO is a command and control man. It's actually the way he is. And, sadly, that's no way to work in a flat business. Time will tell. And I hope he has the strength to prove me wrong. If he doesn't, he'll either have to make way himself – which I can't see happening – or be moved on. Otherwise, all that money, all that time spent by a really talented core of people will go to waste.

I recall a conversation I had with a senior manager of a flabby and lethargic company. This business was enjoying a Customer life of about half its industry average. However, because the sales team was adding new business at a terrific rate, nobody was worrying about the quality of business. Of the total new sales, a little more than half was to replace lost Customers. This business could have been a gold-mine if somebody had taken hold of their bath and put the plug in. The fact was that possibly two-thirds of the orders the salesforce was bringing in were not profitable anyway. They needed to be focused on quality business, to concentrate on building those Customers into a loyal group of satisfied people. Then, this business would have more than its share of miracles. The burning question is why it was allowed to get into this state. The answer this prospective Client gave me was, 'We're profitable. We have new business coming in thick and fast and we're growing. So who cares?'

How does marketing relate to the de-massified infrastructures?

Marketing's major problem is that not only are the businesses it serves fragmenting, but so is its market. It is this added factor that makes the creation of marketing as a central resource less than satisfactory. The problems are as follows.

1. Marketing and sales become distanced (or further distanced) at a time when they need to become closer than ever. Not a miracle in sight.
2. Marketing as a central unit stays just as slow in response time as it always did, in contrast to the other areas, which, as they speed up, will become increasingly frustrated with marketing slowness. No miracles here either!

3. Marketing becomes more distanced from Customers, less in tune with their needs, and hence less capable of predicting the future with validity. A veritable miracle famine.
4. A central resource is less flexible and cannot be redeployed or re-focused easily. Still no miracle potential.
5. The central resource is ill equipped and ill positioned to join in any partnerships, allegiances or relationship building and will therefore not be encouraged to involve itself when, in fact, it has a vital role if success is to be achieved. This is lean on miracles, too.

However, the most significant reason why I do not recommend marketing as a central resource is that it does not suit its role for the future. The future is not simply about putting on single-transaction sales, it is about creating and nurturing long, healthy and happy relationships with satisfied Customers. Marketing is therefore not to be seen or used as a resource. It is, or must become, for a true Customer-driven business, an integral part of your product or service. Nothing less. Now we're looking at a possible miracle or two!

The argument in praise of hierarchies

There is a very lucid case for maintaining hierarchies, not least because they have worked well for so long. Most vocal of the academics in favour of hierarchy is the American professor Elliot Jacques, whose book *Requisite Organisation: The CEO's Guide to Creative Structure and Leadership* (Casson Hall/Gower, 1989) lands firmly on the side of hierarchies for large companies. The only thing wrong with hierarchies, the professor suggests, is that, after some 3,000 years, we have not got them right yet. The part of his argument that I consider to be most valid falls into two areas, which, even though I find my own sympathies lie elsewhere, serve to highlight the danger areas for de-massifiers. They are:

Danger Point 1 – Professor Jacques suggests that flat businesses (or we might call them non-hierarchies) defy human nature. As individuals, we want a pecking order and we want a ladder to climb. He argues that people feel more comfortable, work better and have more career motivation in such an environment. My view is that that's fine, but that people have to change to fit in the changing environment.

Danger Point 2 – Professor Jacques has severe doubts about the way groups, as distinct from individuals, can be held accountable.

In an article published in the 'Harvard Business Review' in 1990 under the title of 'In Praise of Hierarchy', Jacques wrote, 'It (hierarchy) is the only form of organization that can enable a company to employ large numbers of people and yet preserve unambiguous accountability for the work they do.' He concludes the article by writing that 'hierarchy is the best structure for getting work done in big organizations'.

A flaw in this argument may lie in the thought that most users of the fragmentation concept are creating a network of small organizations out of a large one. In my own view, if there is evidence that hierarchies work well in your business, it may be better to break up the business into smaller units and create small hierarchies than to suffer the imperfections and burdens of a large one.

The concept of work groups or teams, a system about which Professor Jacques also has concerns, was considered to be new and innovative even 20 years ago. The notion is that a leader supported by multiplexed disciplined colleagues of equal or similar status is an unproven commodity, yet to me it sounds like the perfect description of a board of directors – a group which I think might want to claim a fairly well-proven case.

Your database – a prime resource

Whatever structure you choose, one of the most important resources for the future is the Customer database. The ability to access information, especially Customer information (or indeed the ability to find the data to process and turn it into information), will become the issue around which all other issues revolve. Information is, in this context, power – it is the future commodity of an integrated business. As both sides – market and marketer – fragment, communications and logistical problems increase, although bureaucracy and waste decrease.

So no great step can be taken towards becoming a Customer-driven business without the ability to move and process information around the network; or, indeed, to provide the built-in monitor, the finger on the pulse, the control systems. A Customer-driven business focuses on improved human interaction. It takes time. It feeds on information. Organizations need to have a core to Customer database operating in real time, or as near to it as possible. Customer-driven processes improve not only the nature of transactions and communications but the quantity of them, whether 'improves' implies up or down. That's where some of the miracles will come from. The database will prove key to the effectiveness of your personal and corporate efforts at building Customer relationships.

Getting closer to Customers

An important realization in getting closer to Customers is that, hitherto, they have not known what they want because they have not known what they could have; they have simply taken the choices on offer. In business-to-business situations, as the relationship succeeds and the boundaries fall, one of the greatest fields for new product ideas, development and proving will be within the joint project work that develops. When Customers get to appreciate the boundless choice available with customization, I expect industrial, professional and commercial progress to speed up tenfold by 2010. The technology is already sufficient to support such a jump. It may even enable us to reach this level earlier.

I'd like to interrupt myself at this point to explore some other side-effects of customization, since they will impact greatly on the structure of businesses. The knock-on effect of customization (indeed, individualization pushes this argument forward further still) is substantial. It is possible to predict a huge decrease in the commonality of the work done by those looking after Customers. In many cases, industrial marketing will become a one-to-one process. There will be massive product proliferation as information networking reveals to other teams within the company the products of the intensified development work. It will, in turn, shorten product life-cycles even further than they have already become under the influence of modern technology.

These three factors alone promote a fascinating insight into the changes that will eventually come to business. They push it closer to integration with the selling role and towards an inevitable conclusion that ISMS could become a very diverse process; it will be almost an individual Customer-by-Customer process for many practitioners. Its primary information source will come from networking with others in the same corporation or syndicate, with perhaps only a modest central resource for strategic counsel and training.

Most importantly, the Customer database must run from core to Customer and, as quickly as possible, the communications decision-making process must be moved to the front line.

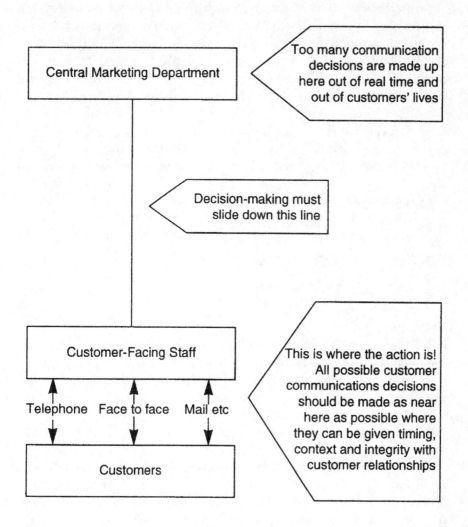

Figure 9.1 Communications decision-making must be devolved to the front line

Customer-driven businesses need Total Communications Management .

Earlier, we discussed the notion that relationship marketing must use integrated communications to move the efforts of the ISMS teams into real time with their Customers.

From the way the signs are pointing, and with the ideas we've been considering, it is quite clear that the existing communications management and control systems are hopelessly outdated, unsatisfactory and inadequate relics of the past. Total communications management is a philosophical concept that suggests that you must organize your communications to reflect and honour the integrity of the relationships that are created with Customers. Otherwise, you might create a magnificent five-star hotel with only one telephone line.

It was suggested earlier that the way you manage your communications presents a shaft of truth to the Customer about how individual and personal their service is. Every modern consumer has experienced this let-down. The moment when one human response to your situation has given you hope of satisfaction – and the next, when a mass-produced missive shatters what seemed like a solution but is revealed as an illusion.

Aspects of structure

Redesigning structures for Customer-driven approach will have an impact throughout the business. No one will remain unscathed or unaffected, but those to whom restructuring should make the most difference are your Customers. Remember again that flatter corporate structures make management and control both harder and more critical – this is where those tight/loose controls come in.

A business operating to tight/loose controls requires that its managers have crystal-clear business objectives to which they must work, and against which their performance will be tightly measured and recorded. However, the ways they may set about achieving their objectives will be subject to very loose controls, allowing them great freedom of decision making, activity, method and, necessarily therefore, responsibility.

Whatever controls are employed, other aspects of dismantling hierarchies are important. Indeed, you can expect to lose some valuable benefits for which you must be careful to make provision in a new structure. For example, how do you harness corporate pride? How do you build corporate commitment? Both these important requirements must be engendered for an effective business that has confidence in its ability and belief in its standards.

Within a hierarchy, these qualities tend to breed quite well, since both the system and the culture enjoys and often rewards them, but this is not the case with fragmented structures or autonomous business units. With these, you have to take positive steps to encourage pride and commitment and to help these qualities grow. This is achieved through performance and communications – anything that can be done to build pride and commitment to the business unit is generally the best first step. It is important that these autonomous units do not become too wrapped up in themselves and, therefore, place all their allegiance and commitment within their own team. They must not lose sight of the fact that they are part of the total business and must maintain high key attitudes to corporate desires and strategies.

Handling information systems

The information systems of the new structure will be critical. And information systems have some characteristics that should be recorded here. It is likely you will already have suffered these in some way – perhaps for many years! But let's recall them anyway.

Computer systems can be essential. This sounds obvious. Indeed, it is. So much so that most people place an expectation on the computer system that is preposterous and unachievable. Computer systems may be helpful – but they are not a universal panacea!

Managers always seriously underestimate the preparation time required, the resources that will be needed, and the costly, time-wasting, frustrating disruption that is created.

Software is always late. Always!

Inadequate thought and effort always go into the disciplines that should ensure data integrity and accuracy. This is always discovered too late, costs too much to correct, and takes too long to become operational. It has been my experience that there is a critical link between the integrity and accuracy of data and its ownership. Data ownership should always be shared by those who provide it and those who use it.

Broadside or network?

The final consideration of this chapter is whether you should deploy your new ISMS teams or business units in a broadside array or as a networked structure. If the units you have created are wholly autonomous, because of their self-sufficiency, go network. A corporate network of small businesses, in fact!

The far-reaching influence of the Customer

The Customer-driven business gospel is not new. It is as old as the hills and well tried and proven. This is an undeniable fact, although, like world wars, thank goodness (and let us pray it stays that way), those who can recall what it was really like are growing fewer in number. For the majority of those in business, it is pure hearsay – or at least it would have been, except for the fact that the true standards and values of the quality regime have been so shunned and spurned for so long, that they have been neither heard nor said.

We have already seen how quantity took over and how and why the pendulum swung so ridiculously far the other way. It is no wonder the consumer is feeling that enough is enough. I suppose the question here then is, 'Why can't we turn back the clock and market like they used to in what can quite fairly in this context be described as the good old days. What has changed?' The answer is 'nearly everything'. The whole dynamics of business are entirely different – the numbers, the speed with which things are required – and the expectation of Customers generally has changed out of all perspective. Moreover, as their just compensation for the exploitation they have suffered, Customers will expect the wrongs to be righted, but will insist on hanging on to the rights that they have gained.

The business world is not made up of idealists and philanthropists; it will only consider accepting the return of Customer issues as long as it can hang on to the quantity. I believe, however, that to a great extent both sides can win with the Customer-driven approach. I also recognize that the corporate structures that delivered quality the last time round would collapse under the strain as today's quantities were pumped into the system. Unfortunately, making them bigger or more robust will not help either, since they then become too clumsy and unwieldy to provide the speed and reactions required in today's business world. Indeed, with flexibility as a keyword to survival for the future, this point would be well taken by today's businesses. Frankly, many of them still operate the same elaborate hierarchies and command and control systems that they operated at the turn of the nineteenth century. The systems have not been built to provide quality and quantity. They have only succeeded with one or the other. So there is a strong argument to look for new ways.

Is it necessary to meddle with corporate infrastructures to become Customer-driven?

Most probably. To a large extent, individual answers here will depend upon the nature of the organization, the nature of the business and the way it interfaces with its markets. Tracking back to the three generations of selling will help us to solve these issues. Consider the first generation and the structure of its sales and marketing division or departments. It has a classic hierarchical shape. From director to regional or branch sales and marketing managers to district sales or product managers through to the salesforce. They operate via the muscular regime. This creed is that to sell more you need more people to sell. Their operating methods are aggressive and highly promotional. Their objectives are singular: to move product. The salespeople work alongside a marketing team where, in the worst cases, a strong sales director will have beaten marketing into subservience, and they will have become a support group providing promotional and marketing services on demand. In the less severe cases, the sales and marketing teams co-operate. It frequently happens without a great deal of respect on either side and, as a result, they don't often seem to like each other very much!

From this we have discussed the evolutionary change that developed with the second generation of selling. The idea was to present a wider spread to the market. It cultivated operatives who had a Customer service mission. This pattern was achieved through simple re-focusing of direction and by closer integration of the sales and marketing effort. Indeed, this regime often became confused, and argued about whose role started and ended where. The second generation is the 'cupped-hands' regime at work. Its operating methods are kind, attentive to Customers and much more service-oriented than its preceding generation. Its creed is service assistance; and its corresponding objective the added-value sale.

Ideas like advertising agencies

Often, second-generation businesses would benefit from building Customer service mini-hierarchies. The mid-1970s to mid-1980s saw a global outbreak of these units like daisies on an early summer lawn. I have always thought that advertising agencies set the best example of this type. Their account-handling structure – account executives, account managers, account group managers, account directors and account group directors – worked extremely well in the context of the big monolithic agency. However, there are danger points.

The first danger point is the way the communications path gets longer as the organization is successful and expands. A group with four account executives, two account managers and an account director can be expanded to, say, eight account executives, four account managers, two account group managers and an account director with relative ease. The problem here is that, as the layers increase, the centres of inspiration and authority in such hierarchies – the leaders – are getting further and further apart. Thus, life becomes an inevitability of small decisions and procedures and protocols that make major decision making tedious, cumbersome and slow.

The second danger point is a tendency to bureaucratic systems, in response, usually, to the volatile, unpredictable and fast-moving nature of the people involved and the work they handle. Those bureaucracies can also become self-fulfilling, with heavy overheads and low productivity, hidden by the amount of work they generate in perpetuating their own existence. It is strange how often these units, in many senses a team, have little, if any, team spirit.

The sales or Customer services units, when looked at in detail, are in fact simply micro-hierarchies within greater hierarchies. Where they are headed by a strong, inspirational leader, they can be very successful. They tend to have executive and operational strata; the operational tiers generally have three kinds of communications functionaries:

the Ambassador – a traveller;
the Voice – a telemarketer;
the Scribe – contact through the database.

There have been massive developments here in databases, and sales direction and management systems are now coupled to Customer communications and transactions by computer. This leads to all manner of cost-efficiency improvements, from increased supervision and management effectiveness to better stock control and resource management. Looking at the Figure 9.2, you can see what I mean when I tell you that this is essentially just a classic service team approach.

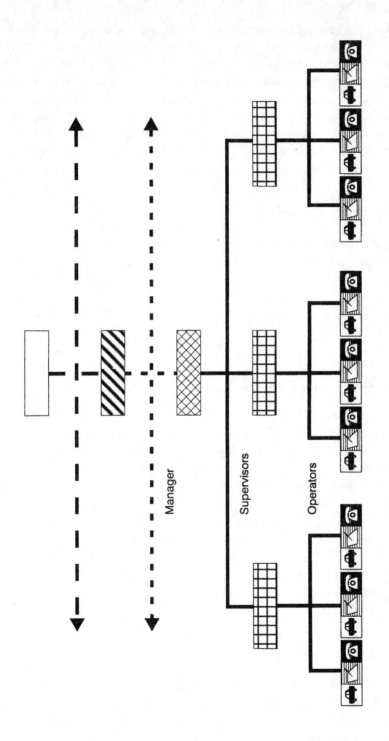

Figure 9.2 Customer service units: hierarchies within hierarchies?

Is the classic Client service team concept dying?

As a solution, the fact is that the classical Client service team concept can still work very well indeed. However, for the future it will work best for those who have found their natural place in the second generation. My belief is that, to move into the third generation, we need to see the creation of a new style of Client service team, and I propose that such teams should work as granules within a broadside structure or a network structure.

What style of team works best?

Staying with the second generation a moment longer, it should be remembered that, when choosing which business style will best suit the teams, the more traditional methods and techniques will work better with the classical Client services team. It is, after all, a hierarchy. It is with the flatter structures that new management styles flourish. Yet, in a hierarchy, rank, authority, and strict procedural ideas about control, transmission of instructions and reporting thrive.

This is not generally a good environment for the experimentation and entrepreneurism required by the third generation. Yet, in the context of individualized product and Customer service, together with a need for increased sensitivity and responsiveness, it is clear why the reservations develop with the conventional first-generation structures, techniques, cultures and management styles. They were fine for the Age of Plenty but are nowhere near enough for the Age of Sufficiency.

The new management style for the third generation is responsible: it can take decisions and be accountable for them. The new style is mature: it understands the need to become more business-oriented. The new style is autonomous, adventurous and challenging: it stands ready to get close to Customers, to find new ways to satisfy their demands, and it constantly questions beliefs, practices and dogma. The new style is alert, free-thinking, strategy-conscious and technologically competent and fluent.

Dear God, please send a new idea!

Having researched this whole area with masses of help and advice, and discussion for more than ten years, and that decade and more now of practical experience with my Clients, it seems that none of the conventional solutions fit. So, the big problem with our third generation (which is a pseudonym for the future of business!) is that it's a renegade. To solve the problem, we need some new thinking.

The thesis of Total Communications Management is simple: in order to ensure the integrity of Customer communications within the relationship (and to overcome the communications traffic jam), one person must be assigned responsibility for the communications of an individual or of a group of Customers. The object of that assignment is to order and adapt both content and timing so that the reality of the Customer relationship makes a difference to the communication being sent. For classical structures, this is as implausible as it is impractical.

Therefore, in order to ensure responsive decision making and corporate flexibility, the responsibility must be devolved to the front line where the action or interaction is happening. Thus, the granular business unit, as I have called it, is born. It operates in the mind, body and soul regime. Its creed is a profitable partnership. Its operating methods are creative, committed and entrepreneurial. Its objective is to expose its brains. It is, inevitably, a self-managed team.

Adopting the granular business culture recognizes the following.

> Buying decisions will involve more specialists. It equips each granule (Customer-serving group) with as many specialists as demanded by the Customer relationships or niches for which they have responsibility.
>
> In the future we will see many more trading partnerships where it is recognized that specialist know-how requires in-depth, intimate work from people who understand the larger issues – and, therefore, where their mutual development path will lead. Such relationships rely heavily on a build-up of mutual experience and are optimized by stability and longevity.
>
> We will see greater rationalization of brand/product/service lines. This must happen to enable the customization that the market will require and the individual treatment and recognition it seeks. We need a unique person to identify and manage the relationship. For that relationship to succeed at maximum effectiveness, we must be able to seem like a small personal business, acting almost as if we only had the one Customer to deal with at any one time. With granular structures such idealistic levels are possible, but they require that, instead of sales or marketing teams, we create small autonomous business units. We are dealing here with a switch from the ability to sell to the ability to cultivate business.

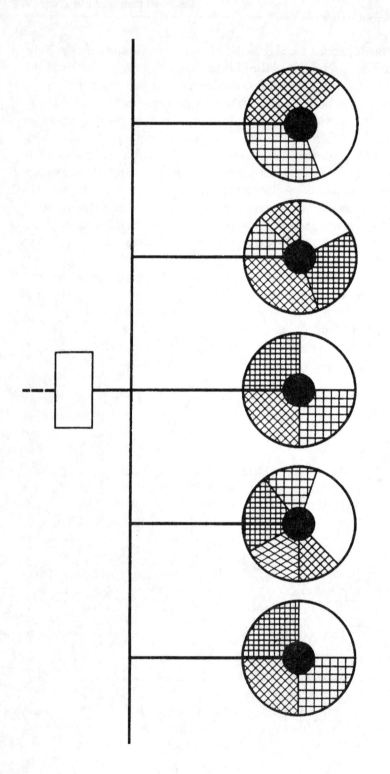

Figure 9.3 Granular business structures

Figure 9.3 illustrates a typical granule; the segment, tones and patterns represent different business disciplines. For example, these might include ISMS, product development, administration and financial. The nucleus in the centre of each group is the leader who takes over-all responsibility for the team's quality, effectiveness, performance and achievements. The segments can represent numbers of people or proportions of specialist resources. Notice that each is different according to the segment or group of Customers it is servicing. When deployed, the picture is as described below.

First, in the forward direction towards the Customer *two* styles of relationship will be cultivated: interpersonal and intergroup.

Second, the exchanges take place via the matched specialists within the marketer and commissioner (Customer) groups.

The marketer and commissioner groups – essentially a deployment for business and commercial interaction – are two matched teams and the reason for describing them as three teams is because each partner in the relationship operates as a team, but they should also all feel part of the same team with common goals. In consumer markets, it could be argued that such relationship arrangements could exist with, say, families or couples. Certainly, there is no reason why the spirit of partnership should not exist. My travel agent, for example, considers herself a partner in my business travel and seems to be as concerned as we are that our holiday arrangements are perfect.

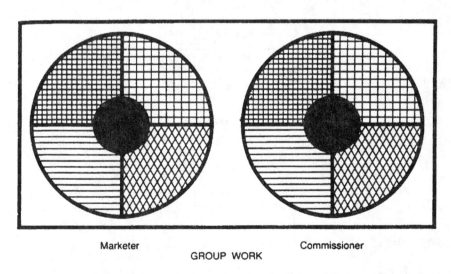

Marketer   Commissioner
GROUP WORK

Figure 9. The marketer and commissioner groups: a total of three teams

Third, the operation, management, analysis and success of each granule is highly database-dependent. Its forward external, reverse external and internal communications requirement are four-fold in nature. They fall into four categories:

information – to provoke inspiration;
demands – to meet the needs of the relationship;
requests – to meet the desires of the relationship;
responses – to satisfy the two preceding categories.

Fourth, the resources of the granule are supported and augmented by two 'banks'. The first is the Know-How Bank, which supplies internal and external specialists. Similar to a centre of excellence, this is a centre of experience, expertise and knowledge. The second bank is the InfoBank – the home of the database.

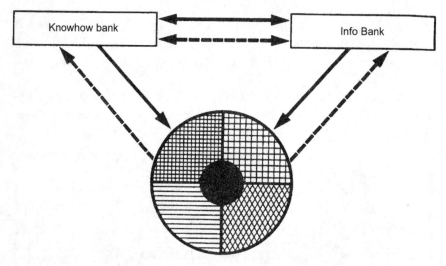

Figure 9.5 The granular banking process

The structure in Figure 9.5 is a triangle and will effectively collapse without any one of its three inter-dependent legs. But the most important part is the two-way banking process. It achieves its ultimate power and strength if the withdrawals do not exceed the deposits!

Here we have a fundamentally important view of the new structure. The structure itself consists of a diverse array of self-managed units, which are, in essence, micro-businesses. However, we also wish to retain the advantages of a large business, while gaining the flexibility, and the speed of response and decision making of a small business. When your business splits itself up into these Customer-oriented small units, something magical happens. Instead of one business trying to solve its problems one way, it becomes a hive of experimentation and differentiation. The results of this must be gathered, retained and shared. If they are, you can imagine how the learning curve is improved. My experience suggests that it will increase almost in proportion to the increase in the number of units. Thus, for example, if the business transforms to become, say, 30 small autonomous businesses, then the learning process can be improved almost thirty-fold.

This has no benefit unless what is learned is stored and shared. Hence the importance of the two banks – the InfoBank and the Know-How Bank. The first is the Customer information, the second is the knowledge and experience of the business. With the benefit of this learning curve, any business will establish and then maintain best practices at the speed of light in comparison with conventional competitors.

There remain three major issues in relation to decisions about new structures: 1) are these units sales and marketing units or complete micro-businesses? 2) how do they relate to each other and to the corporation? 3) and how are the personnel motivated and rewarded?

Micro-businesses or sales and marketing only?

The true product of the future for so many marketers is know-how. They will be selling to the head; it will be an intellectual exercise. This will be true even where, by the classical definition, the product is a manufactured item. I anticipate that, where the business has a product that is manufactured, granules will be primarily ISMS units; although, depending on the nature of the product in question, they should be structured fully to meet all the needs of the Customer that necessitate liaison and exchange. However, where there is no such production base – services and the professions – there are only exceptional cases where these units could not be complete micro-businesses operating with maximum power and responsiveness for their Customers' benefit. These units will effectively combine the best of a small business with the best of a large one. These two methods are illustrated in Figures 9.6 and 9.7.

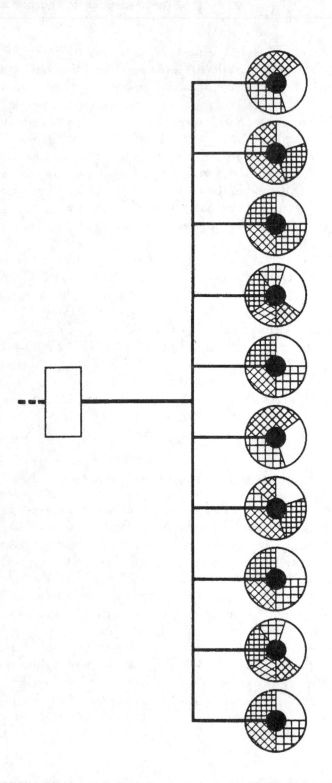

Figure 9.6 A broadside granular structure

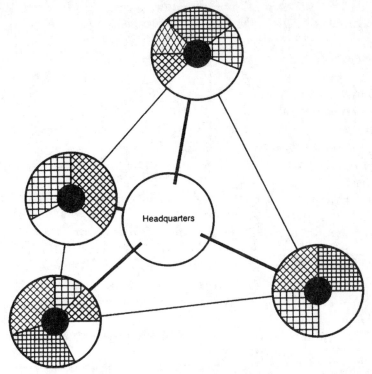

Figure 9.7 A network granular structure

The broadside array in Figure 9.6 has a line-tie to the business centre. Each unit will operate like an ISMS company within a group, even though it will not actually be so autonomous. In the network array, an umbilical cord exists to the core business. This cord carries the banking details, the performance review, goal setting and other central resources. Granules are networked to each other to maintain a leading-edge exchange of thinking and know-how.

What have we achieved?

Let us review what we have achieved by creating such structural changes. Apart from providing the means for optimum relationship building, we can see the following.

The Old Way

encourages individual effort;

discourages consultation and teamwork;
promotes directionally wrong and old-fashioned values.

The New Way

sponsors team effort;
encourages group activity;
provides the forwarding of the total corporate promise;
propagates relationship values;
seeks not merely to listen, but to understand the Client/partner.

Just as the 1980s and 1990s saw the creation of centres of excellence, in the future, marketers will create centres of empathy.

This chapter has dealt with some matters of structure and suggested some new ideas for you to consider. They may not all relate to your business; some may only relate to those you buy from rather than those you sell to and, therefore, help them better to meet your needs. When it comes to corporate structures, one thing is clear – it's all about Customers.

Let me endeavour to summarize the major points:

The distinction between sales, marketing and service is about to disappear. We should assist it. ISMS – integrated sales, marketing and service – is the best solution for a Customer-driven business.

The issue of re-shaping to get closer to Customers reaches to the heart of the organization; as such it is a board issue, not a departmental issue.

The notion that Customer relationships have an asset value will change the power balance of companies and enhance the role and value of ISMS.

There is a dual hurdle in presenting the case to the board: first, the directors must be aware of all the issues; second, they must understand the deep and critical significance of this matter. In other words, this is a matter of corporate life or death.

Corporate structures should be elegant in design and must reflect the needs of the Customer. However, it is foolish to think of this in a rigid way. For the future, structures will become more flexible, and more responsive to Customer needs.

Flatter structures benefit from tight/loose managerial controls, which give clear objectives and firm measurement but greater freedom of action and decision making.

Some benefits get lost when hierarchies are flattened. It is therefore important that specific provision is made for them. Vehicles must be found to harness corporate pride and foster corporate commitment to the total enterprise.

With regards to the planning and implementation of new information systems, the following factors are common:

    systems are helpful but not a universal remedy;
    no computer systems are easy to get in, up and running;
    time, resources, disruption and costs are always underestimated;
    software is always late;
    data accuracy disciplines are never good enough;
    data ownership should always be shared by those who provide it
    and those who use it.

If Customer-driven ideas for relationship building are to be implemented on a departmental basis, a broadside array is recommended; if on a corporate basis, a network structure.

The Customer-driven concept is not new. However, the structures and methods previously used are now inadequate and inappropriate. New ideas must be found.

The idea of increasing the intensity of the classic Customer service unit will continue to operate, for those business methods do not change. However, again, this solution is inappropriate for fostering relationships of the depth and breadth we will see in future.

Teams are the perfect unit concept, however, a Customer-driven business will need a new environment in which to flex its muscles. It will demonstrate a new maturity, which is more business-oriented generally, and more responsible specifically.

The rate of product development that results from customization will create a rate of progress that will compound the innovation rate technology has already created. This has three side-effects:

    decisions will involve more specialists;
    trading partnerships will add intimacy and stability;
    rationalization of brand/product/service lines assists customization.

Whether granules operate as wholly autonomous businesses or as ISMS units only may depend on whether the business manufactures a product or not. Manufacturing or product businesses may choose ISMS units but with vastly increased freedom, influence and authority.

Granules created as ISMS units only should be deployed in the broadside array with a line-tie to the business centre. Fully autonomous granular business structures should form a network array.

10

Getting the right rewards

Your next task is to encourage and reward success; further, where restructuring has taken place, you will need to put back elements that will have disappeared. Remember that, when hierarchies are abandoned for the new flatter structures, one element of the reward system is effectively removed – promotion. The death of the middle manager casts a long shadow! So, there can be no better time to consider the role of pay and reward systems, both as a motivational tool and for nurture and propagation of your Customer goals.

Rewards – how they relate to the corporate mission

When projects such as reorganization or cultural shift are under way, the spirit to drive this through will come essentially from three sources. These are the reservoir of corporate pride, a sense of sacrifice in the common good and, of course, powerful incentives for excellent performance. Such incentives tend to work best when the schemes are simple and cover all employees. Typically, these are geared to different factors, depending on the level of employee. For example:

shopfloor – productivity, unit cost, quality and Customer service-based;
staff;
    related to productivity or cost control;
    meeting Customer and quality requirements;

management – performance against unit costs and/or margins; executives;

> performance related to return on capital employed and economic value-added;
> share options;
> Customer satisfaction and loyalty.

It is vital for pay to follow the culture or mission, not lead – or even mislead – it, in effect, thereby, reinforcing objectives not driving them. Push rather than pull. A danger here is that with some of these issues we forget the big picture. For, if we are embarked upon a Customer-driven mission, or have a quality perspective, this will affect our interpretation of, for example, rewards based upon productivity or cost control. It's not fast and cheap regardless – it's fast and cheap, and perfect for the Customer.

Deciding the objectives of pay reform

Along with the implementation of Customer-driven ideas there are two pivotal roles for our pay and reward system: we want it to assist with the restructuring in some cases, but in all cases we want it to play a long-term and significant part in the transfer from quantity product-driven to quality Customer-driven objectives, and from the hard to the soft issues.

One simple example will illustrate how this latter point is effected. Consider the change that occurs when a salesperson is moved from commission on short-term sales to commission on long-term profits. All of a sudden that salesperson modifies his or her whole negotiating stance, finding new, less aggressive and friendlier, more caring ways to lure. Plainly, this shows that we can achieve our objectives and underpin our corporate changes of direction. However, we need to think how our people, not just our salespeople, but all our people, can be made to concentrate on relationship building.

Before looking at the factors that we can use, perhaps we should consider whether there are any other objectives that should also influence our thinking. As well, of course, as its motivational impact in enhancing corporate pride or commitment and recognizing business, marketing or sales performance, pay reform can also recognize the following:

cost control or reduction;
the attraction and retention of key staff;
changing employee behaviour.

Of one thing you can be certain: it is the business need that will dictate
the direction of change and that means...

...back to Customers, once again

Since the driving force in our decision making is now the Customer
relationship, we can broaden the scope to consider what I call 'geared
motivation'. This has three major aspects. First, it rewards business
growth, not simply sales. Second, it brackets rewards. And third, as
I shall explain, it offers a range of 'gearing factors', which include
more qualitative than quantitative factors.

The concept of bracketing rewards is fundamental to the Customer
mission. By setting minimum levels below which little, preferably no,
reward is triggered, one effectively sets a minimum acceptable performance standard or average. Setting maximum levels inhibits over-
emphasis on aspects that might detract from the declared goals. This
clearly could dissuade those who place too much value on the sales element and encourage them to focus on other aspects of their work. For
example, a salesperson who is paid 20 per cent commission up to 80 per
cent of target, 25 per cent up to 100 per cent of target, and 30 per cent
thereafter is basically going to screw every last sale out of anyone who
steps in his or her path. Volume of transactions will be high, but quality
of business will be low, and repeat business will also be low.

Thus, it can be appreciated that, just as putting on a minimum
bracket means that minimum standards are laid down, so by putting
on a maximum ceiling for reward it is clearly demonstrated that selling to win more commission and to fulfil personal rather than corporate goals is not what is required. The qualitative gearing factors are
now added. Let us take a look at what I mean by gearing factors:

sales;
profitability;
spread of business;
longevity of relationship;
Customer satisfaction;
Customer loyalty;
Customer-loss rates;

share of spend;
problem-free periods;
research results;
initiative;
innovation;
team spirit/activity;
personal spirit/activity.

Of course, you can add more to these to suit your own corporate desires. Your selection of factors becomes the criteria against which employees are measured. However, none of them need necessarily relate directly to sales or turnover (not even the sales factor); they could all relate to corporate performance, however you choose to measure that. The disadvantage here is that the less direct and visible schemes become, the more trouble people have seeing what they have to do.

To be clear about the possibility that the sales factor might not be related to sales, let's take an example – it's confusing when you write it, let alone when you read it! You may choose to give a salesperson a salary, which, on target, is set to provide, say, 80 per cent basic and 20 per cent from incentives such as commission. Of the 20 per cent rewards you have chosen your gearing factors so that actual sales turnover generated will provide one-quarter of that, in other words, 5 per cent of total pay. However, the 'pot' from which the rewards are paid does not have to be a sales-generated one. It can be generated by items that are much more closely related to corporate success. Such a calculation will ensure that the time investment by the salesperson is well thought out, but also that they know that, at the end of the day, a happy, satisfied Customer leads to happy, satisfied employers, which leads to happy, satisfied employees. I said earlier that simplicity was a good quality to strive for in a pay and reward system; it is, but, alas, it's not always so easy to achieve.

Where to start

When setting the pay and gearing factors, it is always easier to start from the amount you want your people to receive when they get the job right, and then work back to decide how your gearing factors will deliver that amount. If you want someone on target to earn £20,000, of which 10 per cent should be performance-related, set the basic at £18,000, then decide how you wish to deal with the rest. For ease, let's say the system will cut in at 80 per cent of target and cut out at 120 per cent. Thus, this employee will not earn less than £20,000 (on target), or more than £22,000. Systems like this can be operated to pay the rewards monthly, quarterly or annually, as you prefer. Now all you have to do is decide on what basis the reward will be allocated.

Describe the job you want done

It is not really possible to consider pay and reward systems without a word about job specifications; the two should be locked together. When you change what you need from your staff, it is essential that the new elements are incorporated into their job specification (and that the old are removed). Each aspect should be discussed in detail with the employee and, where relevant, the correlation with the reward system clearly explained. Where subjective judgement or assessment is to be used (and that's probably in a great deal of areas), the methods of measurement and control must be abundantly clear to the individual employees. Also, they must be just as clear about new operational procedures. As they become more flexible and less prescriptive, there is a growing interest in describing jobs, not just as tasks, but also in terms of competencies.

When preparing the job descriptions, try to remember the 'tight/loose' idea and give people more freedom to move, but in a more tightly defined direction. One way you can prove whether you have constructed these mechanisms properly is to ask each member of your staff to describe to you how they would relate these changes through to each Customer and, therefore, how they will treat that Customer differently. If that is not possible – perhaps because of scale – get them to nominate a representative number of Customers or representative clusters of Customers and then give you feedback in exactly the same way. When they are presented with their new job descriptions, you need to be sure that they understand what they will need to do differently. How will it change their behaviour, decisions, actions, responses and feelings?

When considering the remuneration strategy for your employees, whatever their grade, there are four factors that should be pulled together by pay: the style and culture of the business, the objectives of the business, the structures and societies in which your people work, and, last, but always first in fact, the delivery and satisfaction of what your Customers want and need of you.

Changing systems of remuneration

I don't need to remind you, I'm sure, that pay is a sensitive and emotive issue. In fact, it is remarkably so, and this is always quite confusing when you set it against where employees rate pay in relation to their motivation. In a survey by the UK's Ashridge Management College, employees cited the challenge and interest of the job as their most important motivation, followed by authority and freedom to carry out their tasks. Salary was ranked third, yet it is often the topic about which people will be most vocal and emotive.

Changes to existing systems should be planned and executed carefully. There is no reason whatsoever why one cannot run a transition period for, say, two or three years, achieving one or two steps at a time towards the end result.

Performance-related pay – remember the team too!

If there is a warning to accompany performance-related pay it is that it has been criticized for over-compensating individuals and detracting from their performance as team players. In connection with becoming Customer-driven there is a definite balance to be performed here. In the granules – the self-managed units – it is quite likely that you will wish to team up sales and service people, and measure their joint performance with their group of Customers. So the teamwork aspect should be thought about fully and not diminished or distracted by the scheme you design.

In businesses with many small sites, treating offices as one team can have benefits in encouraging co-operation between employees and the sharing of workloads. People can receive payments for their individual performance as well as for their contribution to the group's achievements. A reference period should be established against which future performance can be judged. The nature of the changes that are required to earn the expected bonus or commission should be highlighted. Modelling alternative options by spreadsheet can provide a simulation of potential events, likely rewards and vulnerabilities.

Even the most dynamic pay packages usually need some form of grading or job evaluation to establish the equity of basic pay. It is common to have regular personal appraisals, not always linked to pay, by which the performance of individuals is assessed against specific objectives. There is currently some interest in upward appraisals, in which managers subject themselves to assessment by subordinates and peers. This is not for the faint-hearted, but it is certainly typical of the spirit of openness that flourishes in self-managed units. To the subordinate, it demonstrates the desire to build an environment of openness and personal development. However, it is important that staff feel secure in this process and appreciate how it can help them to build confidence and stature. For the manager, it provides valuable feedback, consolidates the relationship with the team, and provides fascinating insights into his or her style, and how it is received. The feedback is valuable in checking how you are getting on in your quest to encourage everyone to realize that it's all about Customers.

This chapter has taken a fundamental look at pay and rewards in relation to Customer-driven businesses and described how you can think about what has to come next. In summary:

> When structures are flattened, one of the great motivational factors for employees – promotion – is severely hindered. This focuses their mind on other aspects.
> Rewards should relate directly to the corporate mission. Simple schemes covering all employees are generally the most effective.
> Pay must follow the corporate culture or mission, not lead it.
> The major objectives to be influenced by pay reform are the following:
>> cost control or reduction;
>> the attraction and retention of key staff;
>> changing employee behaviour;
>> enhancement of corporate pride and commitment;
>> recognition of business, marketing, or sales performance.
> Motivational elements of remuneration should reflect the desires of Customers – the issues that are at the root of Customer satisfaction and loyalty. Geared motivation widens rewards from conventional quantity objectives:
>> it rewards business growth;
>> it brackets rewards;
>> it recognizes, measures and rewards the quality and the soft issues.
> Gearing factors can include:
>> sales;
>> profitability;
>> spread of business;
>> longevity of relationship;
>> Customer satisfaction;

Customer loyalty;
problem-free periods;
research results;
initiative;
innovation;
team spirit/activity;
personal spirit/activity.

Job descriptions have a direct link to the pay and reward policy. New elements of the description should be explained clearly to staff and the relationship to the pay system underlined, where appropriate.

Job descriptions should be modified at the first opportunity to give employees as much freedom to move as possible, but in a tightly controlled direction.

When presented with their new job description ISMS employees should be able to prepare a plan (in accordance with their new specification) for each Customer. They should be able to describe precisely how this will change their work, attitudes and feelings. Where numbers preclude this, they should be able to do the same but for a representative sample of Customers or, at the least, for individual clusters of Customers.

Performance-related pay should support team or group activity.

11

Checklists for success

One of the central themes of this book is that in the desire to become a Customer-driven business, no one can be left out, from the doorman to the business leader.

I almost wish that the expressions 'relationship marketing' and 'integrated marketing' did not have the word 'marketing' in them. Yet, unless we create an integrated process of advertising, selling, marketing and service that is focused on delivering one-to-one relationships with Customers, no business can become truly Customer-driven. 'Relationship marketing' and 'integrated marketing' are fundamental. However, this same combination of principle and process cannot succeed without the whole business believing and practising them. Marketing – the marketers or the marketing department – may sometimes be the point at which the conviction, the belief, the initiative, the 'sell' starts, but change must happen throughout. Thus, it simply will not work without the commitment and dedication and energy of the business leader. It really doesn't matter what that leader's title is; it really does matter that they are prepared to re-shape, reorganize, and re-culture their business to dedicate themselves entirely to the Customer.

I have been working on these issues with my Clients many years now. It has been the most stretching, challenging and rewarding time of my life. But I must be honest. I think I have seen as many failures, or perhaps part-failures is more accurate, as I have outright successes. This shouldn't daunt those waiting in the wings. We can usually see quite clearly why ventures were less than successful or did not make the most of their opportunity. The old cliché is proved correct again – hindsight is a wonderful thing. And with other people's experiences and experiments to observe and analyse, when we can learn from negative outcomes or downsides, there is no reason why you need to follow them.

A while ago I was asked to talk at Management Centre Europe's Global Conference on Marketing. My speech was entitled 'Whether to drive your marketing by quantity or quality: a crusader's review.' As I sat writing the speech, I created a catalogue of the failures and enormous successes I had seen in the past. It has occurred to me since that, for your purpose, it does not really matter what outcome your forerunners saw. The successes can be seen as examples and the best ideas can be picked out. Other experiences can be turned to success by learning the lessons that others have gone through for us. Let's just see them all as stones that we can turn over and, under which there may be a miracle waiting to happen.

Inevitably, I am about to summarize and reflect upon much of what has gone before. And for the closing sequence of this book that may not be such a bad thing. However, I want to encapsulate my thinking for you and to pull certain elements together. In my view, there is nothing you will read in the following that, if repeated, doesn't bear the repetition. Let's start with looking at why this book was written – and why I gave the speech that I gave at the Management Centre Europe conference.

Why the crusade?

My crusade is an unashamed attempt to put business back on track. It is born, I suppose, from a meglomaniac, arrogant, passionate belief that I have the answer and that most of the rest of the world has either got it wrong or is only just beginning to see it correctly. 'Correctly', to be quite explicit, means 'my way'! The crusade started in 1985 and will probably continue into my dotage. It is a consuming passion.

What is the crusade?

Having been in advertising, sales and marketing for a period of more than 30 years, some years ago I had a mid-career crisis! I became convinced that marketing was over-obsessed with quantity issues and under-obsessed with quality issues. As a result, from a CEO's point of view, marketing was only helping businesses to 'run the bath with the plug out'. Marketing was returning a very poor ROI; leading businesses into short-term tactical approaches and thinking; causing businesses to suffer lower than necessary margins; and perpetuating inferior Customer service.

Remarkably, the global business world did not notice my mid-career crisis! Many businesses had started to accept that they should be market- or marketing-led. However, one of the most popular interpretations of this – mainly heard from marketing directors or marketing VPs – was that it meant 'Do whatever marketing say and give us even more money to do it with'. The extreme practitioners of this are now mostly out of business or under new ownership.

By 1989, I had become quite despondent – only a few companies seemed to want to follow me down the road of quality. Even though many wanted me to give rousing and inspirational speeches about it, they didn't actually want to do it. It was at this time that I heard Professor Lou Stern presenting the thoughts resulting from his work with Professor Phil Kotler and, as I re-read his speech on a plane from Johannesburg, I decided I now had concrete supporting evidence from two of the best minds in the business. They had, in effect, carried out a decade-by-decade review of 17 different aspects of marketing strategy. Each aspect concluded with a prophecy for the 1990s. It struck me deeply then, and cheered me on enormously, that 14 out of the 17 strategic trends pointed clearly to the necessity of being driven by quality rather than quantity. Out of the way, quantity! HERE WE COME!

Maybe this crusade wasn't going to be so lonely after all. Maybe things were happening at last that would enable me to be re-enchanted with the profession of marketing.

The transition story to date

Years later, it is fair to say there was a business revolution going on and it was happening in some businesses around the marketing department, but, in the more interesting ones, because of the marketing department. It was not only interesting, it was also great fun. There is nothing more fascinating, exciting and adventurous than running along the sharp edge of business practice and experimenting with the future.

Along the way, as I actually got involved with people experimenting in new Customer-focused practices, I realized there were flaws. It was at this stage that I developed the early Customer-driven concepts and realized that this wasn't just a marketing issue. It involved the whole business, and everyone in it. Becoming Customer-focused was a cosy sales and marketing principle – becoming Customer-driven was much, much bigger.

The business revolution in which you may be taking part, or that you may be witnessing, is causing many companies and corporations to suffer severe headaches. But what is truly extraordinary is just how few of the headaches are actually occurring within the marketing department itself and how few of them have actually to do with what, classically, we have defined as the marketing process.

Here's where the major problems occur: at the front line; in IT; in logistics; and with the Customer database. And in the boardroom. And in the CEO's office – a point to which I shall, I must, return later.

To reiterate, Customer-driven marketing works in what I call the 'soft issues' of Customer relationships. It formalizes and brings into the strategic spotlight those things that work most effectively to build and sustain relationships, as distinct from simply working to sell. It builds loyalty. It is quite common among my Clients to have formal work or projects dedicated to such soft issues. They have targets. We measure and analyse our successes and failures.

Incidentally, let's remember here the point made earlier about measurement and Customer satisfaction. I feel that measuring this, while it is often worthwhile and interesting, is vastly over-rated by management generally. This to me constantly proves itself to be an insubstantial and frail statistical measure. Just as satisfaction is an insubstantial and frail quality in Customers. It is easily shattered, easily withdrawn and easily transferred to others. Loyalty, however, because it must be earned and cannot by definition (or at least my definition!) be bought or bribed, is much stronger and more tangible. Satisfaction is fine measured as one of the strands of loyalty, but, on its own, rather misleading. If only because we tend to be self-satisfied with too low results.

The key benefits of building customer loyalty

Let me first run through some of the major benefits that I have seen accrue from a quality-led approach to marketing, which has a clear objective to cultivate, sustain and manage Customer loyalty for the long term.

Improved Customer service – substantial lifts in loyalty here are the inevitable outcome. Often, the whole notion of Customer service is redefined. It becomes an obsession to exceed Customer expectations, not just with every transaction, but with every contact. Only once have I sat with a group seriously considering that it was better to lower Customers' expectations rather than increase the performance delivered. Finally, they came to their senses!

Increased Customer satisfaction – again, it is almost inevitable that significant improvements to Customer service yield significant increases in Customer satisfaction. Not always! One company I went into were busy improving services that the Customer didn't actually want in the first place!

Increased Customer loyalty – as businesses shift away from the short-term objectives and practices of trying to set in motion a chain of single transactions, it enables them to get much closer to Customers and to have a deeper and more reliable understanding of their needs and desires. It enables those same businesses to recognize individuals, to respond to individual likes and dislikes, and to value and demonstrate its understanding of the individuals, families or organizations that are its Customers. Inevitably, this moves greater effort and activity into the 'soft issues'. There is a significant emotional content to such work; when it goes well, both sides feel good, and when it goes wrong, both sides feel bad.

Increased marketing effectiveness – my experience over the years suggests that, when a business breaks its obsession with quantity and successfully addresses the quality issues, it effectively starts down a path that will enable it to improve its sales and marketing cost effectiveness by up to 40 per cent. This can be quite a scary process for traditional or conventional marketers, since they have to accept that the results of mass-media brand building can be achieved in much more difficult, but much more cost-effective ways. This makes their lives hell and does away with high exposure, fun work and glamorous trips and treats. They have to roll their sleeves up! The pay-off is in miracles.

Increased corporate stability – loyal Customers, the natural end product of a Customer-driven business, display two valuable qualities that benefit corporate stability: they are much more consistent, and much more predictable. In times of change, and in times of market volatility, these two qualities have a greatly increased value. Indeed, there can surely be no safer haven, no greater shelter from the storms of the marketplace, than having the most effective possible relationships with your Customers, your own staff, your suppliers and your shareholders. Achieve all four of these and you are about as safe as you can be. Loyal Customers are more dependable; they are more forgiving and tolerant (although I don't recommend that you challenge this too often!); and they behave very reliably. Again, the miracles abound.

Increased profitability and/or decreased or stabilized costs – most businesses I walk into practise high-activity marketing. As they shift over to a quality driver, we move them on to high-focus marketing. High-activity marketers are running the bath with the plug out. High-focus marketing puts the plug in, and it works miracles. Among many things, it affords the luxury of long-term strategic decision making: we can choose between having another bath, having a bigger bath or turning the taps down. High-focus marketing also brings some problems. Politically, it challenges marketing directors and marketing VPs. These people sometimes act as if there were some kind of psychological link between their ego or self-esteem, which is connected to their budget or the number of staff they employ. They also fear that the improvements can't last and that the money, once it is redeployed, will never return. This is a valid fear. My experience suggests that, once the money is redeployed, it doesn't need to return.

These are some of the potentially substantial and significant benefits enjoyed by organizations that are prepared to let go of the traditional approach to business, and to shift into development and management of the soft issues of Customer relationships.

Before we move on to the next batch, I'd like to remind you of something I said earlier:

> It is fascinating to see just how few of the headaches are actually occurring in the marketing department itself and how few of them have actually to do with what, classically, we might define as the marketing process. These problems occur at the front line; in IT; in Logistics; and with the Customer database. And in the boardroom. And in the CEO's office.

As we move on to look at the next batch of miracles waiting to happen, I am sure you will begin to see why this is so. While you reflect on these things, let us also recall that in some businesses quantity and quality are like the North and South Poles – about as far apart as you can get!

The shift from one to the other takes time. I used to believe that two to three years felt about right; my experience now suggests that this is not fast enough and 18 months is more appropriate.

Batch 2 of miracles: Getting rid of the inhibitors

I said that the transformation from being quantity-led to quality-led includes risk: it also requires radical change, experimentation, courage and faith. For the record, I have found that quality-driven, or Customer-driven concepts cannot work in businesses that have the following:

> Command and control cultures – businesses that are scurrying around following orders from the top cannot achieve the Customer focus or responsiveness required to succeed in a quality ethos. They are obsessed with upside-down values and are generally too introspective, bureaucratic and Customer-dysfunctional.
> Centralized marketing decision making – marketing and advertising, as well as selling, have to take place at the front line, or as near as possible to it. Thus, centralized decision making of any of these three disciplines precludes successful work in the soft issues. For marketing and advertising, in the future, this makes a big difference. The task of the central marketing resource is to become a centre of excellence, the guardian of brand and marketing standards and a hyperactive training resource. It must also retain and develop and monitor strategy; indeed, this is a major obligation. None of these is easy when so many other marketing functions and responsibilities have been devolved frontwards. To achieve success, marketing must increase its ability to observe, listen and learn, and it must grow to be sensitive and skilled at the same time.
> Lack of desire to re-engineer sales and marketing – there has to be corporate (not just sales, advertising and marketing) acceptance of the significance of Customer loyalty, Customer superformance and high-focus marketing. These cannot be achieved by the old ways. These are enigmas to the old methods. Thirty years of experience have to be thrown out. The 'baby' and the 'bathwater' both need to go down the drain together. Everyone needs to cheer with full enthusiasm as they disappear, never to be seen again, and the 'plug' should go in the moment they disappear.
> Separate sales, marketing and service teams – to create seamless delivery you must get rid of the seams. Without multi-disciplined

teams of individuals who take full responsibility for groups of Customers, failure is the only end result. Nothing less than an integrated process can be called ISMS: nothing less works to respect and deliver towards one-to-one relationships with Customers. It is not enough simply to rationalize or organize better Customer – or, for that matter, non-Customer – communications, and to say that you have an integrated approach. You only have a semi-integrated approach. In some experiments I have worked on, most Customer teams have also included other disciplines – for example, technical, product development, financial or production – sometimes temporarily, sometimes permanently.

In creating miracles, there is always a great deal of work to be done. Some situations may develop for which we need to be prepared. Following is a list (quite a long one) of situations or issues that have to be supervised or managed while you put your miracles into place. I have called this...

Your list of miracle enhancers and enablers

The Culture Issue

All managers at all levels have to realize what it is like to work in the new culture. Now, delegation is often upwards. To some extent, the higher you are the harder it gets. Your only salvation here is that you can no longer get much higher. There is no height! The hierarchy has gone. But you can get smarter, more widely skilled, and more accomplished.

The Database Issue

For ISMS to facilitate a business to manage Customer relationships, it becomes vital for information to run 'from core to Customer'. The database must run from the strategic centre all the way through to where the business really happens – at the front line. It's a two-way highway operating in real time and has intersections wherever Customers may make contacts, or where Customer information – statistical or actual – may make a difference.

The Speed Issue

Businesses need to implement change with the maximum of speed. The biggest cause of speed failure is not that change takes too long, it is that the decision making and the planning never leave enough time for the work. Change programmes are often doomed to failure before they start simply because lack of vision and lack of courage extend the time involved in creating the vision and planning the change process itself. These become indulgences of hesitation and procrastination. Those businesses with an inspirational leader, strong convictions and a sense of purpose will leap light years ahead of their competitors. More on this to come!

The Communications Issue

All communications need to be handled with thought and openness. Referring to the four-way model, we can appreciate that communications with staff, suppliers and shareholders can be significant in a change process. However, the particular communications to which I refer here, which need to be managed and to have integrity, are Customer communications. They must be pushed into real time and they must make sense to the Customer, and be fully cognizant of the Customer's current status and history. They must equally be in tune with the nature and style of the relationship. It follows logically, therefore, that control over such communications must be placed as near to the front line as possible, preferably right at it.

The Prioritization Issue

Customer service standards should be corporately consistent. However, Customer perceptions of service levels vary, and (this is an important realization) they vary broadly in line with the Customer's actual value to the company. Customer priorities should be set along a 'cost to serve' rationale, which develops the only permissible hierarchies in modern times – these are hierarchies of Customer service levels aligned with Customer lifetime values.

The Experimentation Issue

One of the greatest accelerators of modern business learning is the recognition that an increased number of Customer-serving units or teams gives an opportunity to provide less uniformity. In other words, it offers a greater opportunity for problem solving, and a valuable base for, and source of, experimentation. Sadly, in my experience, even where the need to experiment is accepted, methods are inhibited by fear of risk or by an adverse attitude to it. What we are actually considering here is an attitude to risk. And we need to take more risks, otherwise there will be no gains. Yet, even where managers are able to come to terms with accepting, even welcoming, the gain from taking risks, employees have an innate distrust and dislike of it – their experience over the years has demonstrated that what old attitudes define as 'failure' is career limiting! The learning from both positive and negative outcomes must therefore be extracted and enshrined into new and successful business practice, so that the benefits may be seen and felt. The visibility of the gains neutralizes the guilt and encourages the experimentation process. Above all, the cross-fertilization of shared experiences and shared successes must be ensured. Failure is a negative word and, when applied, so often prevents the adventurous and the innovative from having the courage to take initiative. To categorize a person or an event as a 'failure' denies that any learning has taken place, suggests that no experience has been gained and that no value, at least, can be achieved.

The Motivation Issue

Promotion and money, as motivators of employees, are now of increasingly dubious value. Managers have to find ways to replace them with personal growth and fulfilment, and increased involvement in 'important' issues.

Forget what politicians tell you about 'full employment'. I get very angry when I hear politicians of any persuasion, in almost any country, using those words. The hard fact of life is that unemployment is here to stay. Technology is causing unemployment faster than any improvement in a country's economy can create jobs. This will never slow down; it will only speed up. While, in human terms, this may give many of us cause to reflect on what we call progress, and its effect – and what we think about politicians for that matter! – it is causing those who remain in work to re-evaluate what they deem to be 'career success'.

With no hierarchy to climb, for the enlightened, greed is being driven out, and the creation of increasing value to the business is being driven in. As time passes, this will also – to the delight of most shareholders – probably end what the popular press calls 'fat cat' salaries for 'captains of industry'. Apart from a rich and talented bunch of genuine entrepreneurs, a talentless bunch of grey people at the front of many corporations right now are being paid as if they had built the empire, rather than just finding themselves at the top of it. This situation should shake out and settle back to the right money for the right people as shareholders and employees assert their views.

The Reward Issue

I talked earlier about integrating different disciplines to construct and align multi-discipline teams with Customers. Often, these teams have been motivated by different reward systems. Groups with common goals must flourish when they have common motivations and common reward criteria. It is my experience that, for example, bonus funds may be built from sales activity but distributed for the whole of the Customer-aligned team against service, satisfaction or loyalty achievement. It can be 'paid' out as cash, but is often used much more imaginatively when re-invested in the individuals or for the team.

The Resource Issue

Corporations should only embark upon Customer-driven or quality marketing initiatives from the basis of strength, success and profitability. I have already demonstrated that the changeover from quantity to quality has many strands and, thus, is very demanding of time, energy and money. It therefore follows that the next issue is...

The Reason Issue

Businesses have to go into such complex and risky ventures for the right reasons. They have to believe in what they are doing; they have to commit to the long-term strategy. There is no quick fix here. The switch to quality drivers will not turn round or rescue an ailing business; it is little or no good for anything other than stress and increased workloads in the short term. The 'right' reason is generally a Customer reason, such as developing continuously increasing levels of Customer loyalty by becoming expert beyond competitors at developing and managing successful long-term relationships with Customers. No less.

The Project Issue

I remember having a project definition meeting with a Client in Europe, to examine the necessary projects to establish 'state-of-the-art' integrated marketing. We broke it down into no less than 40 major projects. With another Client, a Customer-focus initiative comprised 84 separate but interconnected projects. Even when key staff are lifted out to dedicate themselves to major project work, I constantly observe other team members suffering stress and over-work through trying to achieve their normal day-to-day goals alongside all that 'vital' project work. This problem is now so widely present that I call it the 'Project Overload Syndrome'. Senior managers will need to watch this conflict carefully, recognizing that the day-to-day work is the lifeline of the business for corporate survival in the short term, just as successful change programmes are their lifeline for the medium and long term.

The People Issue

This has to do with making sure that those who are on-side move forward and those who are undecided or 'anti' move out. You have to be uncompromising about this. Change will only happen successfully if everybody wants it: the moment you start carrying those who are undecided, or who will 'wait to see', you slow the process down and dilute the team commitment. That said, it is also vitally important that the right people are put into the right jobs. Sympathetic replacement of existing staff because they are existing staff rather than because they are right for the job is a dreadful inhibitor – often for them as well as for the business. If people are not happy with the change, they will not be happy with the outcome. Letting them move on in their life, to have the chance of working somewhere else where they can be happy and fulfilled, is the right answer. My advice, even if it is contentious, is to bite the bullet and do it, but do it sensitively and fairly.

The CEO Issue

This has two manifestations: the first to do with gaining support, the second to do with personal power and leadership skills.

> Gaining support: the support that must be gained is that of the – often increasingly institutional – shareholders. CEOs who fail to gain and maintain such support find themselves exposed and vulnerable. There is no way major corporate change programmes, such as a shift from being quantity-driven to quality- and Customer-driven, can be undertaken without the understanding and support of this vital group. The shareholders of successful businesses often do not see the need for major investments and risk-attached ventures. Things are going OK, aren't they? They have the dividends and the capital growth to prove it. 'Suddenly

you want to retain some of it; suddenly you want to take huge sums to do things you never did before, which may not pay back for five years? Why should I support you? And what do you mean you only have sketchy numbers to back up your case? What do you mean it *feels* like the right thing to do?' CEOs need visibly to plan this element meticulously, to stay in constant touch with share-holders, keeping them fully informed. They must be clear about the long-term nature of the task at hand, the competitive advan-tage that is at stake and the costs involved. It is a constant reminder to CEOs that, just as the pressure is now on marketing directors or VPs to supply long-term loyal Customers, so someone has to have the task of making sure that the business also has long-term loyal shareholders.

Personal power and leadership skills: the new management style and culture required by the transformation to a Customer-driven quality set of business processes needs actual demonstration from the top, and huge amounts of powerful leadership. However, the leader in such a culture firmly believes in the old Chinese saying that 'the sign of a good leader is that the people believe they did it themselves'. The kind of leader who can usually fill this role is psy-chologically secure, confident, enjoys justifiably high self-esteem and has obvious charisma and personal power – not to mention being good at the work! These people have realized that leader-ship of a managerially democratic organization is in itself a differ-ent skill, which has to do with motivation through inspiration. I further contend that many leaders of today's Customer-driven businesses will agree with my belief that they have fundamentally to learn to make themselves totally unnecessary to the business but, at the same time, absolutely vital.

It is true that there are many issues (some quite difficult) on that list, which must be managed. However, the scale of each of the benefits they offer remains huge and, indeed, miraculous. The idea of sharing them with you was to highlight them for you, and to prepare you. But you can be absolutely clear about which of these issues has the most devastating potential if not managed – it is the last on the list, the CEO Issue. To attempt a Customer-driven transformation without the heart, mind, body and soul commitment from a capable leader is almost a guaranteed, if not always a total failure – particularly if he or she was not the original source of the initiative.

Finally, a thought or two about solutions

I am learning more and more that solutions cannot be shared, with a view to others using the same ones. Increasingly, it becomes evident that experiences can be shared, but that shared solutions have less and less validity. Tailor-made solutions are the only ones that stick. They are harder to evolve, but much more robust when achieved. I suspect that is why I am seeing increasing Client disillusionment with the larger management consultancies, many of whom seem to hawk round fixed ideas and fixed solutions; a number of them, it could be said, seem to have been arrived at by pirating ideas from academics who are often either notoriously ahead of their time, or notoriously 'head in the clouds'!

Don't be fooled. The action is happening in *your* business. This is where the hands are dirty; where the sleeves are rolled up; where the souls are exposed; where the wounded lie screaming; where the heroes are constantly out there making a difference.

So what of the future?

If you meet someone who can convince you they know the answer to this question, don't believe them, however much you might want or need to. They can only be lying. The great business paradox now is that consultants such as myself are all telling you that you should be striving to get back to long-term values, while experiencing that the long term is a less and less predictable place to be. Despite this puzzling paradox, personally, I remain utterly convinced that the movement is right. How can I be so sure? Because, to a lot of people like you, I am a Customer. And so, to a lot of other people, are you. As Customers, our time has come. Because the business world has realized. It's all about Customers.

In this chapter we have covered much ground and vital issues: they can be summarized as follows:

A number of major benefits accrue from becoming a Customer-driven business:
improved Customer service;
increased Customer satisfaction;
increased Customer loyalty;
increased marketing effectiveness;
increased corporate stability;
increased profitability;
decreased or stabilized sales and marketing costs.

Some things stand in the way of a change programme designed to turn a business into a Customer-driven corporation:

command and control cultures create contradictory dynamics with the change-centralized marketing decision making, which block the move of Customer communications and, therefore, prevent the relationship from moving into real time. The marketing department must become a centre of excellence, the guardian of brand and marketing standards, and a hyperactive training resource;

lack of desire and fully corporate commitment to the re-engineering of the sales and marketing process and organization;

separate sales, marketing and service teams defy the delivery of seamless Customer attention because they perpetuate the seams.

There are some enhancing and enabling issues that must be carefully controlled and managed in order to support and facilitate the change programme and process:

cultivation, education and acceptance of the new management culture;

plumbing the database from 'core to Customer';

having sufficient vision and courage to speed the shaping and planning stages of the programme, so they do not detract in time from the implementation, or delay its start;

accepting that communications should adhere to the four-way marketing model and that, whereas all four dimensions are important, Customer communications must have integrity from the Customer's viewpoint. Not only should they be in real time, but they should also reflect the nature, style and state of the relationship;

establishing the right priorities for Customer service levels per Customer. Levels can vary according to values. Standards should always be consistent;

encouraging experimentation – turning the fear of failure into the joy of learning by enshrining the lessons into best practice as speedily and as visibly as possible;

understanding that human and team motivations are different in flatter, more democratic organizations, and that money and promotion are of decreasing significance; often of increasing significance are involvement, personal growth and development and 'being able to make a difference';

groups with common goals and purposes flourish best when rewarded with common motivation and reward criteria. These, in turn, have to reflect the achievement of Customer objectives;

corporations have the optimum possibility of success when embarking on transformation projects from a healthy state, and with sufficient resources;

change programmes of this nature succeed best when they are initiated for the 'right' reasons. This means they are not a quick fix or a trendy gimmick, but a genuine long-term commitment to Customers. Strong conviction and desire build commitment and energy. The 'right' reason is generally a Customer reason;

project overload is an increasingly frequent occurrence and the balance between investing people in the short term and taking them off-line for dedicated project work needs thought and monitoring;

the vessel of change has no spare places on board. Uncompromising but sensitively handled action is recommended to make sure that the whole team is fully committed, passionate and obsessed by the desire to succeed. 'Don't knows' and 'maybes' dilute, damage and delay change, and are a burden to their business;

by far the greatest enhancement and enablement of Customer-driven change comes from the business leader. CEOs need to gain support from shareholders as well as from their teams. The long-term nature of the change must be accepted, and value placed on the ethical and philosophical benefits to business practices as well the huge profits and the productivity benefits from sales and marketing. A leader who is personally psychologically 'together', with high confidence and self-esteem, will prove the most effective sponsor of change and will facilitate the progress democratically, believing that 'the sign of a good leader is that people believe they did it themselves'. Such a CEO will require that they become unnecessary to the business, but absolutely vital. By this I mean that, for the process and content of the work, the business should function without you. It will continue to flourish. However, you are there for its motivation, energy, enthusiasm and spirit. And for guidance, support, inspiration and entrepreneurism.

Business solutions are becoming less valid and reliable for sharing and cloning for others. Tailor-made solutions are increasingly the only ones that stick.

12

The should you, shouldn't you bit

The road to becoming a Customer-driven business is long, hard and paved with hazards and conundrums. However, as you have seen by now, it's a good road, a worthwhile road and, most of all, an exquisitely profitable road in the long term. All you have to do is get it right.

Well, maybe it's more of a tightrope than a road. We're as far as we can go down the quantity end and we've got to get back along to the quality end. Whichever way you picture it, the questions that must be in our minds now are: Should we do it? Indeed, why should we do it? How much of it should we do? What's in it for us if we do, or don't? Let's consider the answers.

Should we do it?

There seems little doubt that the business world, indeed, the world at large, accelerated by the usual charming forces of human nature – greed, envy, lust and fear, and so on! – seems set to continue along its precarious path. Only faster. When you look at the power balance and the spread of material resources, and the quantity and geography of who has and who hasn't, there is little short-term good news, globally speaking. So, as it always has been and always will be, life is full of spice, interest and intrigue. We must get on with the job. But increasingly our jobs will have to do with the provision of safety and security.

That's why it's important that we understand that we can only deliver quality to our Customers if it keeps us healthy and provides for our own welfare and well-being at the same time. Becoming Customer-driven is not a philanthropic issue; nor even at this stage a moral issue. In this context, it's an issue of commercial survival and success.

The concept of four dimensions of marketing lashed to the objective of relationship building is the practical formula that provides the vehicle I have unearthed for survival, stability and success. Thus, we must look next at what is needed to build and nurture our all-important relationships.

I maintain that there is little difference between the needs of a Customer relationship and those of a personal one. They're both fun, rewarding, satisfying, fulfilling and damned hard work to get right. Perhaps that's why, corporately, so many people are busy screwing each other – in the Customer world, we make corporate love!

So what qualities must we supply to our Customers, along with our products and services, to build the relationships we need? Trust. Respect. Integrity. And affection. These are the kind of ingredients that build relationships. Why should corporate relationships be any different? In my view, the more number crunching, data processing and electronic transfers happen, the more these human values will move into focus. The more robots, computers, machines and systems we devise, the more those things that win the business will revolve around the people. The electronics and the technology after all only breed short-term distinctions or competitive edges. In the long term they are levellers. Ultimately, success and prosperity remain people issues. Importantly, it must be understood that quality is entirely a people issue. Quantity only builds immediate sales. Quality builds friends for your business. Friends yield greater quantities, and for longer – arguably, this is the biggest potential miracle we can make.

Reading the signs

You can see this happening already. Businesses, drowning under the expectations placed upon them by their Customers, and pushed relentlessly forward by their competitors, are looking for friends. People to help. Partners. And people to share and commit to each other. Customers appreciate those who get closer and more intimate as the service standards reach levels of excellence and customization never before achieved.

Intimacy, getting close, even making corporate love, were not words or notions used in business a great deal in the decades of quantity. In those decades they called me an 'expert'. Now they tell me I'm a 'Guru'. So is all this Guruspeak, idealistic lunacy, or is it what's going to happen?

On that issue, I will leave you to make up your mind. After all, by now you know a lot about mine! All my marketing and management experience and the years of research and work that have gone into this project convince me the Customer-driven movement is not one you can stop – nor is it one you can ignore. It is a movement that will, over the coming years, obsess all honest, professional and ethical businesses. You can make your mind up about the rest. Just as Customers will.

A compelling business issue

When I put myself in the place of a prospect considering two competitors, I ask questions. Of course! But not just about the product or services or back-up, or country of origin. I ask increasingly probing questions. After all, I am looking to be able to trust and respect these people. Finally, I ask myself this fascinating question:

Do I want to do business with…

A COMPANY THAT PAYS ITS PEOPLE TO EXPLOIT ME?

Or do I want to do business with…

A COMPANY THAT PAYS ITS PEOPLE TO SATISFY ME?

This is one of those questions to which you know the answer before you even ask it. It comes as a simultaneous bolt of lightning. It is a question Customers in droves will ask. They already are. That's why financial services people in an increasing number of countries now have to reveal their commission levels with certain contracts. That's why, as an old-fashioned commission-driven quantity salesperson, I would pray I didn't come up against anyone from Rank Xerox. This company pays commission to its salespeople based on the levels of Customer satisfaction and loyalty they stimulate, rather than on how much kit they can offload on to them. How would their competitors fare in answer to the two questions that preceded this paragraph?

You have no real choice about whether you accept the Customer-driven concept. The world will force it upon you. The questions are, when and to what extent? For as well as considering what the acceptance of the Customer-driven and quality ethics in relation to your business says about you, you must also consider what choosing to ignore it says about you.

Is being a Customer-driven business good for you?

Perhaps this is the more interesting issue. Is being Customer-driven actually good for us – or is the Customer the only winner?

I believe the answer is 'yes'; emphatically 'yes'. It is good for us. Very good indeed. Which is just another pressure to push us all down an inevitable channel. At the end, both sides win. The Customer wins. But they were supposed to anyway. And businesses win. At least, the ones who get there first do.

I explained earlier about the 'quality lock'. It locks Customers to you. It locks competitors out. For that is the nature of business through relationships not transactions; that is the result of being a Customer-driven business where the end product of your business model is a high level of Customer loyalty.

It gets worse before it gets better

Three qualities are necessary to make the switch to becoming a Customer-driven business: time, courage and money. You need the money to invest in the re-introduction of quality standards, ethics and thinking; you need time to plan and implement all the changes that need to be made; and you need courage to do it and to stick it out.

The fact is that, as you make the transition, things could get worse before they get better. This is why the ideal time to make the switch is when you are in a position of strength, and when things are going well, rather than when you feel you need corrective or panic measure in the hope of a boost to business. It doesn't happen, it *can't* happen like that.

However, this apparently simple change of process – concentrating on what we do *for* Customers rather than what we do *to* them – needs careful thought. For managers planning change – Step 1: know where you are; Step 2: know where you want to be; and Step 3: understand the gap – quantifying the curve of 'decline-plateau-recovery' will be all-important. Success will depend on critical analysis and control of these factors; if business will, as it does typically, drop, how far will it drop, how long is the plateau, how high will it climb, and at what rate or angle of ascent?

My experience suggests that there are other scenarios. Business does not always go down before it goes up. I have had a case where we managed a complex change process and kept business at the same level. And very proud of ourselves we all were! And, in one rare case, the solution included pumping up the old quantity first, before instigating the change, since it was the only way we could sustain the momentum and keep the business in business while we got the miracles in place.

While the numbers and monetary values should be calculated and included in the case put to any board in support of the Customer-driven case, it is important that the benefits are fully considered. That is not just the profit, or ROCE (Return on Capital Employed) figures, or whatever your yardstick, but also the fact that, in hard times ahead, you will be keeping yours while all about are losing theirs!

I have also worked with one courageous business, as I mentioned earlier, that decided to go ahead with the change programme I had proposed without any real end numbers to go on. They proceeded with a £39 million set of projects because 'we know it is the right thing to do. It brings our activity in line with our promise. It means we will live our mission statement.'

What will be the engines of the Customer-driven movement?

I shall certainly be one! But what will be the key mechanisms that enable the changeover? I see them as follows:

   harnessing technology, the development of hybrids and the welcoming of IT people to marketing;
   the acceptance of the need for, and provision of, TCM (Total Communications Management) and moving communications control and decision making to the front line and as near as possible in real time;
   the integration of marketing into a fused strategic ISMS process;
   the realization by the Customer of his or her absolute power, and his or her experiments with that power;

the overwhelming evidence that, in the business climate of the immediate decade at least, quantity goals will do more harm than good.

The need to make fast, urgent decisions

Many of the business and economic pundits are forecasting the forthcoming years to be years of chaotic change, and with relentless rapidity. Certainty is a diminishing value. There is no such thing as safe, they say.

I disagree.

Safe is achievable, but it has to be worked at. Becoming Customer-driven is the work.

Those companies that survive, let alone succeed, will have taken far-reaching steps to be sure they can weather the storms. Many of them can be seen to be doing this right now. In this context it is possible to predict the factors that will build resilience and durability. They are as follows:

Flexibility
Can you re-shape, re-group, re-plan, respond and react with intelligence and alacrity?

Team spirit
Do you encourage and reward commitment and effectiveness throughout the business?

Understanding
Listening is not enough. Seeing, hearing, and caring are vital too. Is your company ready to go for share of market achieved by share of mind?

Obsession
This goes beyond dedication, commitment, and service. Because the obsession is with perfection. Also it is possible to single out the key elements for the survival of your business – those things that will unlock the Customer-driven door for you.

Cultural
Can you transform your market and your ethics to the know-how and information-based era?

Method
How soon can you restructure, re-educate and re-align towards multi-discipline business teams?

Style
How fast can you successfully adopt a 'relationship orientation', complete with the prerequisite database capability?

Don't doubt the urgency or the critical nature of these factors. Nor question their validity. Those who already know, who already understand, who already accept, are way ahead of you.

Come on! It's Miracle Time!

Finding the miracles is relatively easy. It's making them happen that stretches us. But when they do happen, the effects really are miraculous. Not just for the Customer, but for everyone. Inside, the business morale leaps; happiness, fulfilment and satisfaction soar; and commitment, energy and drive reach new peaks. These are businesses in which it is difficult to get people to go home at night as opposed to the kind most people work for. That transformation is a miracle too!

Over the years, we have already seen miracles happen in companies throughout the world. We have seen some of those companies thrive. And, some years later, we have seen them fall back to being also-rans. Just look at the helter-skelter ride of IBM since 1985. Brought to its feet by CEO John Akers 'taking his eye off the ball', it was reorganized and restructured into seven so-called autonomous business units, which should have been 70! Billed as the 'largest Customerization in the world', costing $2,420 million, or $2.58 dollars per share, the initiative also knocked $1 billion off IBM's expense rate and reduced the payroll by 50,000 staff. It further re-trained and re-assigned 60,000 people, of whom about half were moved to positions directly involved with developing, making, marketing or servicing Customer solutions.

I told the IBM story more fully in a previous book, yet, by the time the manuscript had gone through the publishing process and hit the bookshop shelves, 'Big Blue' was in trouble again – global business commentators were talking dramatically but earnestly as if it was about to sink without trace! Just for the record, at the time of writing, IBM still exists and seems to be surviving. I expect it will be around for a while! But whether it is on the way up or on the way down remains to be seen, and will probably depend on when you look!

What does this tell us? IBM put itself through the hoop, cost its shareholders a bucket of money, and then performed a miracle, only to find that it needed another one. This happened partly because its initiative had some fundamental flaws, and partly because, while its people had their heads down getting on with this change programme for five years or so, some rat snuck out, tip-toed over to the goalposts and moved them. Life moved on.

Here's the point. Here's what the IBM story tells us. For me, there are two real lessons: the first is that in business today, if you want to stay ahead of your competitors, you need one miracle after another. The old days when you could make a miracle and live off it for the next five, ten, or more years are gone; they have disappeared in the proverbial sands of time. In almost every area of an organization, miracles – some big, some not so big – have been popping out of the bag for a while. If you are going to go prospecting for miracles, my advice is to ignore the old miracle fields, which have been mined for so long, and start looking where you know they're sitting, just waiting to be found. There, nobody has yet stumbled on any. It's still relatively virgin territory with rich pickings. It's marketing and sales.

The second lesson we can learn from the IBM story is that you cannot rely on the goalposts being in the same place when your change process matures. You use your car headlights dipped for the short and medium view, but every now and then you need to put them on 'main beam' to check the long view. You need to do the same in business, in order to check the validity of the long-term outcome. Otherwise, that goalpost-moving rodent might tip-toe out to confound you too!

I've decided. This Customer-driven stuff is not for me!

Abandon hope all ye who feel this way. I beg you to take it as read that you must join the rest of the business world and embrace the Customer-driven way. Not only as your approach to work, but, more importantly, in how you think about Customers.

The fact is that most organizations spend too much money on advertising and marketing. They shower money on prospecting, which every honest person knows is wasteful. They shower money on brand advertising, often with totally inexcusable waste. It is as calamitous as it is ironic that the conquest business and the prospecting still dominate spending and strategy, while returning the lowest possible value that can be obtained from the marketing unit of currency.

During the last 30 years, as a result of misguided and greedy thinking, sales, advertising and marketing have become high-speed, high-cost businesses. They are technologically backward and, in many ways, a decidedly inferior corporate investment. This will not change unless you and I do something about it.

To the smaller business I say this: we talked at the very beginning of this book about the craftsman, a one-man business who cannot see any difference between his craft and the Customer's need. Ask yourself why so many big businesses are trying so hard to break themselves down to become a network of organizations just like yours! It's because you are the perfect organization to be able to get close to Customers, to work with them, to understand their needs and respond quickly. One of the greatest accelerators of the Customer-driven business concept is the envy that so many people have of the effectiveness of the small business in these respects. A small business generally is never allowed to forget the fact that it's all about Customers.

Lastly, may I say something to you, whatever the size of your business, whoever your Customer is, and however you feel about Customer issues. I'd like to thank you for taking the time to make friends with these ideas. I hope they'll serve you as well as the statement at the beginning of this book has served me. It has been my personal approach to business since I was grown up enough to have one.

Thank you for joining me on this wonderful, challenging and, I hope for you, provocative and stimulating journey into the mind of tomorrow's Customer. On which note, perhaps I can leave you with one final thought. It's overleaf...

THE CUSTOMER IS A HOLY COW
YOU DON'T MILK A HOLY COW
YOU WORSHIP IT

References

Peters, T J and Waterman, R H, Jr (1982) *In Search of Excellence*, Harper Collins, London

Frederick Reichheld (1996) *The Loyalty Effect*, Harvard Business School Press, Harvard

Elliot Jacques (1989) *Requisite Organisation: The CEO's guide to creative structure and leadership*, Casson Hall/Gower, New York

Index